THE HUMAN PRESENCE

THE HUMAN PRESENCE

*Ecological Spirituality
and the Age of the Spirit*

Paulos Mar Gregorios

AMITY HOUSE
AMITY, NEW YORK

Published by Amity House Inc.
106 Newport Bridge Road
Warwick, NY 10990

© 1987 by Paulos Mar Gregorios

First published by the World Council of Churches, 1978; Indian
Edition published by The Christian Literature Society, Park
Town, Madras 600 003, 1980.

Library of Congress Catalog Card Number 87-72246

ISBN 0-916349-14-4

Contents

Preface

When several years ago I wrote the pages which follow, I was not as sure as I am today that the human crisis becomes more and more acute with every passing month.

The affairs of the world are largely in the hands of people who are expert at making money, waging war, and playing politics. Our age is characterized by the absence of true charisma among the leadership of the nations and churches of the world. Even what at first seems to be an exception turns out on closer analysis to be the same game — money, war, and the politics of national or group self-interest.

The chariot of human development has gained momentum but seems to be running amok without a charioteer. No one seems able either to stop it or to get it back on course. We know that consumerism is bad, but what can we do except go on consuming more and more? We know that the gap between the rich and the poor is widening, but what can we do except live with guilt and lend an occasional hand to the poor? We know that our vision of reality is defective because of too much reliance on science and technology, but what alternatives can we develop other than an odd and unsatisfying jumble of mysticism, astrology, and communes? This sense of powerlessness is paralyzing.

We know that our civilization needs reconstitution, but civilizations are not made out of whole cloth by planners and engineers. We have to make a gigantic effort to move from where we are towards where we ought to be going. But it has become difficult to be sure in which direction to move, because the vision is not clear, the fog is dense, and something has gone wrong with our eyesight as well.

What follows is little more than an attempt to rub the eyes — it won't restore the eyesight or dispel the fog. Spiritual eyesight can be restored only with the return of moral health, and clearing the fog requires spiritual penetration. But it is important that people begin talking about how the eyesight has been lost and what caused the fog.

The book is a plea — a plea for a community effort. The future does not promise charismatic individual leaders who will take us to our destination. It is more reasonable to hope for charismatic international communities that pioneer and pilot in the interests of humanity as a whole. The Church of Jesus Christ is a community set within the human community. We need now charismatic communities cutting across the borders of church and world, across the confines of each separate religion or secular ideology.

One clue to what causes the fog and dims our eyesight is our conception of the relation between God, man, and the world, and our understanding of what role humanity plays between God and the world. It is towards a fresh understanding of that role that this book is working. The theological position taken is somewhat conservative, or rather, one that seeks not so much to conserve the classical Christian insights as to recover them and reapply them in our context. For the author of this book, to be radical means to go back to the roots. It is for the roots in the Christian patristic tradition that this book is searching, in the hope that if we could put some fertilizer there, the tree might do better and not quite wither away and die. The search for these roots is set in the context of the current crisis of both ecology and technology. There is also a crisis in economics, and the eventual outcome of this book should be the search for a new economics — the economics of engineering a higher quality of human life. That search should be undertaken by economists, scientists, and prophets together. What is attempted here is merely to locate a point of orientation on the horizon, despite the fog and the bad eyesight.

Man is a mediator. He is poised between two realities — God and the world. He shares in both, he is united to both. He cannot live apart from either. That is the meaning of the incarnation of Jesus Christ. The only humanity that can survive is the new humanity, the humanity that has now been inseparably, indivisibly united with God in Jesus Christ. And because of its locus in the one divine-human nature of Christ, the new humanity is a mediating humanity—a humanity that reconciles and unites God and the world. It is an incarnate humanity—a humanity that is an inseparable part of the whole creation and inseparably united to the creator.

This, then, is the meaning of the human presence in the cosmos. To be with the one who unites. To be in Christ, uniting the divine and the human, the creator and the creation, the transcendent and the immanent, the spiritual and the scientific-technological. To enter the mystery of "Christ in us", yes, in us Christians but also in us human beings, in us as an integral part of the whole creation.

The subtle art of image making for the future needs skilled craftsmen as well as the gift of the Spirit. The various crises of our time should be used neither as occasions for doom-saying pessimism nor as a chance to peddle empty-hope optimism. Every crisis is a judgment, a call to see where things have gone wrong and to seek to set matters right, both within our consciousness and in society.

The environment crisis, the economic crisis, the crisis of justice, the crisis of faith, the employment crisis, the monetary crisis, the crisis of militarism—all these are symptoms not only that humanity has to yet become what it has to be, but also that it is on the wrong track.

This book, a humble attempt to provide a point of orientation, owes much to many thinkers whose ideas fill its pages. It owes much also to Dr. Paul Abrecht of the World Council of Churches, and my many colleagues on the WCC's Working Committee on Church and Society. An even greater debt is owed to the library of Gregorian University in Rome where most of the work was done, and to the Pontifical Commission for Justice and Peace who helped me liberally. My thanks are due also to Peter Scherhans and Audrey Abrecht who did most of the editing. Christa Stalschus and Audrey Smith did most of the typing and putting things together. Many others in Rome and Geneva who helped must go unmentioned.

CHAPTER ONE

The Problem Posed

David Lyle suggested that "the human race has, maybe, thirty-five years left".[1] A slight exaggeration, you may respond. Yet we smile rather weakly at the joke. Who knows? Maybe the wolf really is at the door at last. We have always trusted the experts to find a way out. This time, however, at least some scientists and technologists tell us that they cannot handle the problem facing humanity today. So perhaps John Cobb's question, *Is It Too Late?*,[2] is too pointed for comfort. Is the issue nothing less than human survival on our planet?

It looks that way. For Cobb's question is not merely rhetorical. Yet it is not meant to strike terror or to drive us to despair, but rather to provoke us and quicken our will. It may not be too late. But we have no time to waste. Action must be so immediate as to leave very little time for reflection.[3] Reflect, however, we must — and not only the experts. The dimensions of the problem are so immense that all the resources of all humanity must be brought into play.

In this book, we shall ask two questions:

1. What are the elements in the present impasse that raise this question of human survival?

2. What resources can the Christian tradition bring to the eventual coping with the issues raised by this impasse?

1. THE PRESENT IMPASSE

Only a giant leap of the imagination can project on to our mental screens the immensity and radicality of the impasse now confronting humanity.

Worldwide poverty is a burning issue; such great social inequalities cannot long endure; justice has to be enforced not only within, but also between, nations. Our planet is one, and no part of it can go on living in comfort at the expense of others. All peoples have the right to work creatively; all have the right to live with dignity and freedom; all have an equal right of access to the world's resources. The huge disparity in the rewards for work in various parts of the world cannot continue. And world culture must be rich and diverse; human beings should be able to create in freedom, not in conformity with the demands made and the fashions set by one part of the world, or by one part of a community.

To meet these demands would require putting an end to economic colonialism and to cultural imperialism. These two tasks have been bequeathed to us by the age of European expansion, which, on the positive side, has led to the possibility of the world becoming a single interconnected unit. And these two tasks are neither small nor simple. They will demand strenuous effort and a fertile imagination — for many decades to come.

But we are referring here to something even bigger and more radical — the end of an epoch in human history, an epoch whose creative springs go back to the great spiritual upheaval which began 400 years ago. The European Renaissance, the Protestant Reformation, the French Revolution and the Industrial Revolution were all part of this upheaval. Modern science and technology are also integral to it. Bacon and Descartes, Saint-Simon and Karl Marx, Kant and Freud, Livingstone and Vasco da Gama — these were some of the bright luminaries of an epoch that is now ending.

A great creative burst of imagination engendered this now dying epoch, and only a fresh burst can create a new epoch which will endure for a few centuries. The paradox of our present impasse lies in the fact that precisely when science and technology have provided us with the means (but not yet the will) to eradicate world poverty and to spread justice worldwide, the very existence and development of that science and that technology are being called into question.

No extended documentation is necessary to demonstrate the point. The most provocative milieu for the debate was created by the Club of Rome's Report entitled *The Limits to Growth*.[4] Its preposterous conclusion, emerging from one of the most complexly programmed computer research projects at the Massachusetts Institute of Technology, was that the only viable model for an earth which would survive beyond a few decades would be one in which both population growth and economic development would be frozen at the present level. This ridiculous formula has been lampooned as a new gospel which claims that the salvation of the world equals ZPG – ZEG (zero population growth plus zero economic growth).[5]

The Club of Rome Report isolates three major problems which converge in the "growth crisis":

a)   the exponential growth rate of population;

b)   the alarming rate at which the nonrenewable resources of the earth are being depleted;

c)   the degradation of the natural environment of human life by pollution, erosion, urbanization, etc.

The debate that has ensued has shown the deficiencies in the programming and therefore the invalidity of the solution proposed. Nevertheless, those who have studied the problem do admit that the crisis facing the human colony on earth is unprecedentedly alarming. The wolf *is* at the door, finally. But after all, if it is only the wolf, we can still do something about it. If we don't we can, of course, very well be devoured.

There are those, like Hermann Kahn in the USA, who till yesterday were reassuring us that the wolf is no problem and that technology will soon invent the right kind of rifle to kill it. There are others, and not necessarily in Africa, Asia, and Latin America, who say that all the pointing to this wolf is only a way of diverting attention from the real problem — international economic injustice.[6] The experts will continue to dispute for years to come on whether the question of human survival on our planet, of the continuation of our race beyond a few generations, is as acute as some claim. We cannot wait for the conclusion of their debate, for time is of the essence. There is enough documentation to enable those who are sufficiently informed and sensitive to realize that we should now begin to ask ourselves afresh the question about the meaning of human existence and the quality of life we want to promote on earth.

There is growing awareness among many that the goals of society as we now conceive it are inadequate, and so in need of thorough revision. Is it not a fact that at present our social goals are:

a)   maximum and ever-increasing production and consumption of goods and services;

b)   optimum justice in the distribution of these goods and services and in the opportunity to participate in making the decisions about production and distribution?

Precisely these objectives are now being questioned as a result of six interrelated factors:

a)   the appalling manner in which efforts to achieve international economic justice are resisted by the powerful and privileged minority (e.g. the failure of the UN's Development Decade to approach its target; the failure of the United Nations Conference on Trade and Development);

b)   the growing realization that we have been thoughtless in the exploitation and consumption of the finite resources of our planet;

c)   the slowness of pace at which humanity is realizing its own oneness and the interconnectedness of its life — or the persistence of parochialism;

d)   the gradually deepening conviction that the individual is not purely or even primarily an economic and political being, and that "having" does not ensure happiness — disillusionment with consumerism;

e)   the yet unconfirmed suspicion that what humanity has been doing to its environment in the last couple of centuries, if not arrested in time, may lead to the suicide of our race or planet;

f)   the trend towards an undermining of our confidence in science and technology as omni-competent; the increasing intensity of the charge that our kind of science and technology is responsible for the impasse in which we find ourselves.

Survival is not the central issue, especially for Christians, who believe that history has to come to an end some time or other. For humanity, the perennial enemies are sin and death—death of the race, death of the planet, and personal death—or evil and loss of being. But these are precisely the enemies which have been faced and overcome by the cross and resurrection of Christ. Christians today live to affirm and advance the opposites of sin and death—that is righteousness and life, or, in philosophical terms, *the good* and *being-becoming without threat of nonbeing*. We can face the impasse calmly and without panic; but this does not absolve us from the responsibility to join the fight against the powers of darkness and death. We have to identify these powers in a fresh way, name them, challenge them, and overcome them, for Christ's victory commits us to continuing battle with them. And Christ has, through his Church, commanded us to overcome evil by good, death by life. We need not only to call evil by its name, but also to work with God to create the good.

But the impasse does exist. The exaggerated language of the rebels should not disconcert us. As Don K. Price, retiring president of the American Association for the Advancement of Science, once coolly remarked:

> The rebels are right in being pessimists...I do not think they are pessimistic enough. To me it seems possible that the new amount of technological power let loose in an overcrowded world may overload any system we may devise for its control; the possibility of a complete and apocalyptic end of civilization cannot be dismissed as a morbid fancy.[7]

Yes, the times are apocalyptic. There have been many such in the history of humanity. We have survived them. But our apocalyptic age demands that we not look back with detached calm, but rather recognize the future as foreboding and therefore act in the present in a creatively new way. We dare not take the comfortable and lazy line: "We have been through many such crises before; we will muddle through this one too."

2. CHRISTIAN RESPONSIBILITY TODAY

It was science and technology that gave us the power to do such great damage to our planet. Eventually science and technology may enable us to repair that damage. The thesis has been seriously advanced that the Christian faith, or perhaps the Judaeo-Christian tradition, bears major responsibility for the dangerous direction in which science and technology have developed in the last couple of centuries. It is, in any case, an uncontestable fact that they did advance by great bounds in the Christian West. Lynn White's essay on "The Historical Roots of Our Ecological Crisis"[8] touched off this debate on Christian theology's responsibility for the violent assault upon the physical environment has led to the present crisis. Others, like Paul Ehrlich, regard our "blind science and technology and [our] berserk econocentric culture" as outgrowths of a Judaeo-Christian heritage.

We shall not pursue in any detail this thesis attributing to the Judaeo-Christian tradition, especially to the Western branch of it, major responsibility for the fact that science and technology are "so tinctured with orthodox Christian arrogance toward nature that no solution for our ecological crisis can be expected from them alone." Indeed, we are glad to accept that last part of Professor White's statement — that Christians alone cannot provide a solution for the ecological crisis — since, after all, they were not alone in creating it.

Christians should not hesitate to accept responsibility for two different attitudes towards nature, both equally opposed to the meaning of the incarnation. On the one hand, Christian asceticism, probably under the heavy non-Semitic Oriental or Hellenic influence from Buddhism, Zoroastrianism, Neoplatonism and Stoicism, has tended to devalue matter and the material world. More characteristic of our time is the tendency to view nature as purely an object to be known and used for our own purposes.

The roots of this second approach are not to be sought in any theology of dominion over nature. Even the theology of work once passionately advanced by Calvinism can be held only partly responsible. The deeper roots lie in the historical phenomenon of the expansion of the West, a phenomenon dating from the Crusades, and developing in the form of world trade, colonialism, and imperialism. Without any rancor or claims to innocence, could we not ask whether greed — sometimes naked, sometimes clothed in highly moral terminology, but always acquisitive — was not one of the factors that led Europe to expand, first for purposes of trade, and then to colonize the rest of the world, to exploit its raw materials and its markets, and thereby to accumulate the capital necessary for building up the industrial system?[9] Greed, which has traditionally been associated with aggressive power and deceptive cunning, motivated both the exploitation of the world and the maintenance of control over its primary extractive industries and its markets. Only the communist system has effectively challenged the march of colonialism and imperialism, and the power and cunning of the latter bid fair today to buy off even that strong contender for world power by coopting it into the market system. Moreover we should not forget that it was this civilization, whose basic ingredients were greed and power, that gave impetus to and made possible the growth of science and technology in the West. Our Christian Confessions of our share in the guilt of exploitation would be more genuine if we acknowledged this fact.

Even from the perspective of both Eastern theology and the exploited two-thirds world, it is impossible to dissociate oneself from Western Christianity and Western culture and society and to brand "them" alone as responsible for our current crisis. Deviations in theology have occurred in both East and West. Greed and aggression are by no means limited to the latter; the need to overcome them is as acute in the two-thirds world as in the West. In fact, our efforts to eradicate poverty and to usher in a just society are frustrated mainly by our own insatiable greed and group aggressiveness among ourselves.

The purpose of this book is to restate the problem posed by ecology for humanity and its life on earth, and to indicate certain lines along which fresh investigation and reflection may be undertaken.

Conrad Bonifazi, a Congregational pastor teaching at the Pacific School of Religion in Berkeley, California, is one among many who have undertaken to provide a fresh biblical theology that opposes "the momentum of orthodox Christianity in its devaluation of the natural world".[10] By orthodox Christianity, Professor Bonifazi does not mean specifically Eastern Orthodox Christianity. Yet the perspectives of that ancient but living tradition also need to be brought into the debate, not as opposing Dr. Bonifazi's "word"-theology, but as a different manner of approaching the same set of problems.

Such an Eastern Orthodox perspective cannot be exclusively biblical nor made-to-order for the purpose of "reinstating the concept of the natural". Eastern theology has always depended for its source on the whole tradition, expressed in the life of worship, in the Bible, in the writings of the fathers, in the decisions of the councils, etc., but always as a living and never a closed tradition. Our conclusion may not be at all the "reinstatement of the natural". We shall seek rather to explore the relationship God-humanity-world, and see what the results of that exploration imply for our present crisis.

CHAPTER TWO

The Nature of Nature

1. THE CONCEPT CLARIFIED

The paradox in our present ecological crisis and our conception of nature has been ably brought out by Gordon Kaufman.[1] Nature has been and is being transformed by human cultivation, human technology, and human culture. But humanity forms an intrinsic part of this nature, if nature really means the sum total of all beings and processes. Human culture in that perspective is part of nature. The paradox refers to the conflict between the inclusive and the exclusive view of nature. Some writers, like Frederick Elder, claim that it is the exclusive view that has led to the ecological crisis, that the Christian tradition is strongly exclusive and is therefore responsible for the crisis, and that only an inclusive view holds out the possibility of survival for humanity.[2]

Once again we seem to be heading for a false set of alternatives on which we can debate furiously without coming to any conclusions. Does the concept of "home" imply only a furnished house, excluding the people who live in it, or is it an inclusive term which takes them into account? The question is ridiculous, for the answer depends entirely on the context in which the word "home" is used. Similarly, even if we accept a view of nature as including humanity, there will still be some contexts in which only the exclusive view will make sense.

It is the very concept of nature itself that is problematic. Human culture and history are certainly part of the ongoing process of reality. The question is whether nature is the right term to describe the sum total of this reality including humanity, or does the very term amount to a distortion of that reality?

In modern usage, there are several sets of meanings for the word "natural" or "nature".

a)   In ordinary secular language, "natural" is opposed to contrived or artificial, that is, something which happens or comes into being without human intervention. We could say that the reference here is to the "laws of nature" or the "order of nature", which operate independently of human intervention. This is nature as the realm of unalterable physical laws, nature as given.

b)   In modern Western languages, nature has come to have a related second meaning — the nonhuman part of creation. When we speak of the beauty of nature, or of caring for nature, we do not mean the order of nature, but rather the visible aspects of the creation around us. But this concept excludes the man-made elements. For example, the city, or at least the complex of buildings, bridges, tunnels, and highways made by human beings, does not form part of nature; rather it is made up of the elements of earth, air, water, and sky, together with plant and animal life.

c)   In Christian theology, nature has two other meanings.
i) "Nature" is opposed to "history" and "culture", which are the realm of human action. Protestant theology since the 19th century has tended to emphasize the action of God in history as the central revelation, while usually underplaying his visible activity in nature. The concept of natural revelation has seemed dangerous, since it may justify the knowledge of God in other religions.
ii) This Protestant distinction between "natural revelation" and "special" or "historical" revelation has its predecessor in the medieval Roman Catholic distinction, still current, between nature and grace, or between the natural and the supernatural. Grace is God's special and direct action, while nature is given, and has its own laws. Grace can counteract, supplement or overcome nature; it comes from outside or from above nature, and hence is qualified as supernatural.

d)   Underlying all the above meanings of the word "nature" is another: the given structure or constitution of a person or thing. It is not in the nature of a cat to fly. The hawk and the wolf are by nature cruel. Here the reference is both to the given behavior pattern and the expected character of an entity.

We shall have occasion to refer later to these four meaning-contexts,[3] but it will be useful to analyze here the assumptions behind them.

First, the various usages of the word reveal very important metaphysical assumptions. Would it not be correct to say that the Western classical world-view has a more sophisticated three-storey universe than the much lampooned ancient three-tier structure of hell, earth, and heaven? At the lowest level of this three-storey structure is nature as an order with its own given constitution, for both the whole and its parts. On the second level stands humanity, creating culture and making history through its actions. On the top level is the realm of the special actions of God, to which terms like revelation, grace, and the supernatural refer. Let us call this total structure nature-culture-grace. Under culture, we would include not only history as economic, social, and political action, but also science and technology.

The modern ecological debate seems to be concerned with what the second tier does to the first. The new sin, condemned in strong language like "earth-rape" and "terricide", is what we as a human race have done and are doing to "nature". Civilization is attacked not only as a flight from nature but as a brutal and unfeeling assault on it. No overt reference is made to the realm of grace, though demands for a theology of nature or for an ecological theology are often heard.

2. NATURE IN THE BIBLE

We need now to clarify the concept of "nature" from a theological perspective. The Hebrew tradition is often accused of having desacralized nature and thereby paved the way for its pillage by humanity. But it is a striking fact that that tradition has no word at all for what we call nature. An examination of the Greek Concordance for the Old Testament[4] confirms that the Greek word for nature, *physis*, occurs only in the later books produced outside Palestinian

Judaism in the diaspora living under Greek influence, that is, in the Book of Wisdom and in III and IV Maccabees. These books are regarded as apocryphal by Protestants and others, and do not even appear in the Protestant Old Testament, which follows the canon of Palestinian Judaism.

In other words, it could be said that the concept of "nature" is totally alien to the Hebrew tradition as such. Those who have too easily credited the Old Testament doctrine of creation with making it possible for Western civilization to know and control nature (a totally indefensible claim, in any case) should note that the Hebrew had no notion of something "out there" which they were to set about "desacralizing" and then dominating. The command of Yahweh in the book of Genesis was certainly not "to dominate nature", but only to "be fruitful and multiply, and fill the earth and master it, and have rule over the fish of the sea and over the birds of the air and over every living thing that moves on the earth" (Gen. 1:28). Mastering the earth and all life on it need not mean mastering "nature" as a whole, which is a much wider concept.[5]

This is to say that, in the Old Testament tradition, nature is not conceived of as an entity to be dominated. In most instances, even in the Apocrypha, the Greek word *physis* is not used to mean nature in the sense of the nonhuman part of creation or the whole of creation. It is worth quoting as an example IV Maccabees 5:5-8. The book is an apologetic tract glorifying the defense of Judaism against the encroachment of Hellenic culture. The context of the passage is the cruel though courteous demand of the tyrant, Antiochus Epiphanes, to the venerable Jewish high priest, Eleazar, that the latter save himself from torture by eating swine's flesh, which is forbidden for him by the law of Moses.

> And Antiochus, looking on him [Eleazar] said, 'Before I allow the tortures to begin for you, o venerable man, I would give you this counsel, that you should eat of the flesh of the swine and save your life; for I respect your age and your grey hairs, although to have worn them so long a time and still to cling to the Jewish religion makes me think you no philosopher. For most excellent is the meat of this animal, which nature has graciously bestowed upon us, and why should you abominate it? Truly it is folly not to enjoy innocent pleasures, and it is wrong to reject nature's favors. . .'[6]

Clearly, it is not the Hebrew who says that nature gave us the pig. Only someone with a Greek education could make this statement. Eleazar's reply contains the word "nature", but he uses it in the sense that God has compassion on the weakness of human nature. Even in this pseudoepigraphical work, composed under the influence of Greek culture, the Hebrew uses the word "nature" to denote only the God-given constitution of humanity, not the nonhuman part of creation. In all the other instances where *physis* is used in the Greek Old Testament it has this same meaning.

The New Testament, also produced under heavy Greek influence, still makes but sparing use of the concept of nature, and only in the classical sense of the God-given nature of an entity. James 3:7 and II Peter 1:4 are clear instances of this. St. Paul also uses the word *physis* with this meaning. He speaks, for example, of the "natural branches" (τῶν κατὰ φύσιν κλάδων) as opposed to branches grafted on (Rom. 11:21, 24), or of the Gentiles, not having the law, by their very nature (φύσει) doing the things of the law (Rom. 2:14). For St. Paul, "by nature" could mean "by birth", as when he speaks of "you who are by nature Jews" (Gal. 2:15). But the basic meaning is that of "constitutive nature", as, for example, in the reference to the service of those who by nature (φύσει) are not gods (Gal. 4:8). In fact, St. Paul even thinks that "nature" itself (ἡ φύσις αὐτή) teaches us that it is not very laudable for men to wear long hair (I Cor. 11:14), though very pious Greek and Slavonic monks and not-so-pious moderns defy this teaching. The reference in Ephesians 2:3 to those who are "by nature children of wrath" is a bit more difficult to unravel, for if nature is what is given by God, it is not easy to see how people can be destined to his wrath by the very fact of their origin. But nowhere in the New Testament does the word "nature" refer to the whole of creation or to its nonhuman aspect. That, it seems, is a Hellenic legacy in Western Christian thought.

3. NATURE—AN INDO-HELLENIC CONCEPT

Though the concept of nature itself is basically Aristotelian in its early Greek provenance, among the Stoics it received a currency and value not given it by Aristotle. Nature is the Stoic equivalent of the soul of the world, the *pneuma* that animates it, the seminal logos entirely immanent in the world. Aristotle had not used the word "nature" in quite that sense; for him the cosmos was animated by (ensouled) and had within it the principle of movement.[7] Thus, for both Aristotle and the Stoics, nature itself was a God-substitute. They used the terms synonymously,[8] but for an immanent, self-animating principle in the universe—not for the whole of creation.

The key concept used by the Stoics—the idea of the *anima mundi*, world-soul—is much more ancient among the Greeks than are Plato and Aristotle, both of whom also employ it. It is likely to play a large part in our own thinking in the near future, for ours is also a God-less world, forced to concede that its own existence and processes need some explanation. As the technological crisis deepens, we will need more and more vitalist interpretations of the universe. Bergson, Whitehead, and Teilhard may come back into greater currency, because all three are essentially vitalists operating with a concept very similar to that of the world-soul.

The idea of the world-soul has affinities with Hindu thought also, though the precise concept of a *lokatma* or *prapanchatma* (world-soul or cosmic soul) is hard to find in the rich Hindu tradition. The idea of the ultimate self or *paramatma* in the Upanishads, however, is not far from the notion of a world-soul, nor is the idea of the inner self (of the world) or *antaratman* to which the *Katha Upanishad* refers,[9] and which it identifies with the human soul itself:

> The inner self of all things, the one controller
> Who makes his one form manifold—
> The wise who perceive him as standing in oneself,
> They, and no others, have eternal happiness.[10]

In fact, all the Upanishads seem to use this concept of the world-soul, always, however, identifying it with the ultimate soul of God and the personal soul of the finite individual. It is usually conceived in relation to a transcendent Brahman, until we come to the Samkhya system of Hinduism, which is basically nontheistic or atheistic.

Even the Gita, which belongs to a later period than the Upanishads, maintains this clear tradition of a transcendent universal self immanent in the universe as its soul. In the great self-manifestation of the ultimate universal soul through Krishna to Arjuna, the latter saw "the splendor of that exalted being" as "if the light of a thousand suns blazed forth all at once in the sky".

> There the Pandava [Arjuna] beheld the whole universe, with its
> manifold divisions gathered together in one, in the body of the God
> of Gods.[11]

This concept of the universe as the body of God received central importance in the Hindu tradition with Ramanuja (11th century), and even in Madhva (1197-1276) the organic understanding of the world is still fully dependent on a transcendent God.

A nontranscendent system, parallel to that of the Stoics among the Greeks, occurs in the fully orthodox Hindu system of Samkhya, which is now drawing the attention of many Westerners. The Samkhya system is also noted for its theory of organic evolution, though this is stated only as a rudimentary insight and not as scientific theory. Even more noteworthy in the Samkhya system is the reduction of all categories to two basic entities: person (*purusha*) and nature (*prakrti*). This corresponds to the basic dualism of all empirical knowledge between knowing subject and known object. *Prakrti* or nature is a force, not a static being, having within it various grades or levels of qualities, *gunas*, constituting a progression. These qualities in their interaction produce the world-manifold. But the highest level of evolution of *prakrti* takes place only when *purusha* — the conscious person — excites it and leads it on to its own progressive unfolding.

This school of Hinduism, which flourished around the 7th century B.C., is much older than Plato, Aristotle, and the Stoics. Unfortunately, the earliest Samkhya writings to which we have access date only from the 3rd century A.D.[12] Dismissing openly and completely the concept of God or Isvara, the Samkhya philosophy makes nature or *prakrti* the producer of this world, through the manifold combinations of the various constituent *gunas*.

Thus we see that "nature" is essentially an Indo-Hellenic concept, especially in the sense of an impersonal entity confronting man. In both the Hindu and the Hellenic tradition, "nature" in this sense becomes a necessary concept, particularly in systems that do not attribute the existence of the universe to the activity of the one God. Greek paganism was basically atheistic. Its gods were in most cases only exalted human heroes or personified cosmic powers. The concept of nature functioned as an originating and normative principle, in the absence of the notion of a God who created and sustained the cosmos. The same is true of Hinduism. It is only in the atheistic system of Samkhya that "nature" in the sense of the nonhuman part of the universe comes to play a central role.

It is therefore not surprising that the concept of nature as the nonhuman part of the universe became prominent in the Western tradition only in its post-Renaissance, secularist phase, when the centrality of God began to give place to anthropocentrism. Goethe, Wordsworth, and Shelley belong essentially to this phase, though none of them was openly atheistic. For Goethe, converse with nature was a way of perceiving the *Urphänomen* in it, but he was angry with the technological culture which did not know the right kind of converse to have.

In this sense, there is a dialectical ambiguity in the present revolt against technology and the preference for direct, unitive, reverent perception of and communion with nature. Both the scientific-technological approach and the romantic-unitive attitude to "nature" as the counterpart and companion of humanity hide the basic truncation inherent in that artificial construct of reality which belongs to the classical Western Christian tradition, that is, grace-man-nature. The first aspect becomes almost nonoperative in the confrontation between humanity and nature in post-Renaissance Western culture, particularly in the Enlightenment. This idea should be developed further; we simply note here that nature as the nonhuman part of creation plays a more central role in perception and poetry when the first aspect — God's grace — becomes recessive.

4. NATURE IN THE WRITINGS OF THE FATHERS OF THE CHURCH

The fathers of the Christian Church, true to their Greek genius, make free use of the concept of nature.[13] When, for example, Origen speaks of the unbegotten nature of God (Τήν ἀγέννητον τοῦ Θεοῦ φύσιν)[14] or of the "super-substantial bread" being con-natural to rational creatures,[15] and when St. Gregory of Nyssa refers to God as by nature incomprehensible,[16] they are using the word with its meaning of constitutive nature, and we shall make but scant reference to these. The fathers do make frequent use of the term *physis* in this sense; Mark the Hermit capped off the discussion by distinguishing between what is according to nature (κατὰ φύσιν) and what is above nature or super-natural (παρὰ φύσιν).[17]

We are concerned here with the fathers' reflection on nature in that other sense of the word: the whole of creation, sometimes including humanity, sometimes not. But in this connection we should turn from the word *physis*, or nature, to the words *ktisis* and *ta panta*, both of which mean the whole of creation. The fathers have a strong sense of the laws constituting the nature of all things, but in general they do not call the creation "nature". There are, however, some exceptions to this. For example, the whole creation is referred to as *physis* in Tatian.[18] In later Greek writings, such as the anathemas of the Council of Constantinople in 543, the universe is called the "whole corporate nature" (πᾶσαν τήν σωματικὴν φύσιν).[19] But more often than not, when the fathers speak about creation, they use ἡ πᾶσα κτίσις, the whole of creation, or simply τά πάντα, "the all", everything that is.

It is clear in St. Gregory of Nyssa, who laid the foundations for later Christian reflection on the subject, that the basic distinction for patristic literature is not between humanity and the nonhuman part of creation, but between "He who truly is" (ὁ ὄντως ὤν) and "the things which merely exist" (τὰ πάντα). The two do not share the same mode of being, and to apply verbs like "is" or "exist" in the same sense to both God and the creation seems to Gregory to be disastrous.

This is important, if rather obvious. The fathers were never able to keep their terminology sufficiently clear, even when they were aware of the distinction between the being of God and the existence of creation. They applied the word *ousia* or "being" to both. St. Basil and St. Gregory, his younger brother, both spoke of *physis* (nature) or *ousia* (being) as parallel entities,[20] and John of Damascus in the 8th century systematized the parallelism.[21]

Valentinus Apollinaristes in the 4th century actually identified *physis* and *ousia*.[22] Eusebius of Caesarea (4th century) held that each reality had an intelligible and a sensible aspect, and that *physis* refers to the intelligible and noncorporeal, while *ousia* refers to the particular existence which is seen in change and decay as a corporeal entity.[23] He was, however, philosophically unsophisticated, for when the Christian writers refer to the *ousia* of God, they do not mean a corporeal entity subject to change and decay. Gregory of Nyssa, only a few years later, gave a more defensible definition of nature: "nature" or *physis* was that in which the existence of beings was comprehended.[24] But, here again, he was not referring to the *ousia* of God, since he held this to be incomprehensible. St. Maximus the Confessor (6th century) went the same way in asserting that, in patristic writings, *physis* and *ousia* are similar and have common features in meaning.[25]

Late in the 7th century, the concept of *physis* took on more precision as the identifiable qualities of a class of persons or things, while *ousia* referred to simple existence. John of Damascus said that some non-Christian philosophers made a distinction between *physis* and *ousia*. For them *ousia* meant "simply being" (ἁπλῶς εἶναι), while *physis* referred to the "mode of being" (τὸ τοι ᾦσδε εἶναι) which made possible the classification of beings into species and genera.[26]

5. HE WHO TRULY IS AND THINGS WHICH MERELY EXIST

Greek pagan philosophy had already used τὸ πᾶν, "the whole", to refer to the universe;[27] τὰ πάντα, "all things", emphasizing its diversity (rather than the singular which stresses unity), was rarely used.[28] However, with the 4th-century Greek Christian fathers, the plural came to be preferred. On the one hand, the fathers were reluctant to ascribe total unity to a universe which participated in the sin of humankind, and, on the other, they wanted to reserve the singular for "He who truly is" (ὁ ὄντως ὤν).

The relation between τὰ πάντα, the diverse universe, and ὁ ὄντως ὤν, "He who truly is", in patristic writing seems much more sophisticated and defensible than many modern and classical views whose effort to resolve the distortion in the humanity-nature relationship by dealing only with these two categories does not stand up to profound philosophical testing. Plato had already used ὁ ὄντως ὤν for true existence[29] as contrasted with the passing, changing, shadowy being of the particular existents. Athenagoras of Athens, one of the early Christian apologists, had referred to God as "that which truly is" (τὸ ὄντως ὤν-neuter), as single in nature *monophyes*, and as pouring forth the good from it, as the very truth.[30] Clement of Alexandria also frequently used this expression for the being of God to denote that He alone has true and fully dependable being. This coincides with the Hebrew tradition's insistence on God as "He who is and who will be what He wills to be".

In contrast with this concept stands τὰ πάντα, the changing being of all that has been created. It is this great insight, and not the "desacralization of nature", which stands at the heart of the Judaeo-Christian tradition. God's being is *sui generis*; it is without beginning and without end; it is neither spatial nor temporal. In other words, it is exactly the opposite of created being, which had a beginning and which must end; which exists in space and moves from beginning to end in time. Created being is inseparable from change; it is subject to evil and therefore will inevitably disintegrate and die. Created being which has overcome evil must continue to change, moving towards that perfect good which is the being of the creator. Since we cannot undertake here an exhaustive study of the relation between God and creation—one of the central insights of the Judaeo-Christian tradition—we shall center our study on one writer, St. Gregory of Nyssa, making some reference to others. But first we must look briefly at some aspects of the late Western tradition.

In conclusion, certain preliminary observations can be made on the basis of the foregoing:

a)   the concept of nature as the nonhuman part of the universe is primarily Indo-Hellenic in origin and becomes particularly prominent in an alienated society, that is, one which has lost its direct sense of dependence on and derivation from God;

b)   if the reaction against the evils of a technocratic civilization leads merely to a romantic reaffirmation of and reunion with nature, it cannot be salutary, for even the classical Western Christian tradition insists on the centrality of the third element—God;

c)   in the Judaeo-Christian tradition, there was no such process as a desacralization of nature because, in it, not only was the concept of nature as subhuman creation unknown, but also nature was never "divine", since it was not God but only a created reality.

CHAPTER THREE

Nature and Science

1. SCIENTIFIC THOUGHT: FROM WHERE TO WHERE?

a) Medieval philosophy and the concept of nature

We cannot afford today to neglect or regard with contempt medieval European philosophy. The very roots of the scientific technology which seems to provide the ideological basis for our contemporary civilization go back into that age when Charlemagne laid the foundations of both medieval philosophy and the Western Christendom which was shaped by that philosophy and by the Carolingian Renaissance.

The Europe that Charlemagne inherited was not only broken and divided: it was also deeply immersed in ignorance and superstition. A half-breed paganism — not that of classical Greek civilization, but one which eclectically put together primitive European animism and some Christian ideas and convictions — gripped the minds of the people of that time. The Christian clergy were the medicine men of this magico-religious cult, misguiding the morals of Europe and clouding its intellect.

Charlemagne founded schools everywhere. He had a double purpose: to dispel the ignorance and superstition that lay like a shroud over Europe, and to build up an elite corps of literate civil servants through whom he could hold the continent together, for the benefit of the educated classes, namely, the clergy and the nobility. Later, these schools were to shape and sharpen the European mind. The scholastic hair-splitting that so amuses modern students was the price to be paid for the development in European culture of the intellectual acumen which would be needed in the future to stimulate the growth of science and technology.

The father of medieval philosophy, that enterprising Irishman, John Scotus Erigena (ca.810-ca.877), went in 847 to the most famous of these early medieval schools at the court of Charles, King of the Franks, in Paris.[1] The concept of nature played a central role in his thought. However, for him, *natura* did not mean the subhuman elements of the universe, but rather comprehended the totality of all processes and beings, not only humanity and the world but also God and the universe. It was a reality embracing all — God-humanity-world — in eternity and time. He divided all beings into four types of nature:

i)   *natura creans et non creata*, or nature creating but not created (the unoriginate and *sui generis* nature of God, which is above the good);

ii)   *natura creata et creans*, or nature both created and creating (the archetypal world of ideas, created by God, and giving rise to [creating] the world of particulars);

iii)   *natura creata et non creans*, or nature created but not creating (the universe of humanity and the world which has no creative, but only fashioning and begetting power);

iv)   *natura non creata et non creans*, or nature not created and not creating (the final *apocatastasis* when all creation will have attained perfection and be united with and in God and all creative movement will have stopped).[2]

This strange fourfold classification of nature, which envisaged a growing, developing universe that would become static only when it had attained perfection, makes it possible to regard John Scotus Erigena as a forerunner of the modern process philosophers.

The strongest influence on this Irishman was beyond doubt the thought of Dionysius the "Areopagite" whose entire works he translated from Greek to Latin,[3] faulty as his knowledge of Greek seems to have been. The Greek manuscript was a gift of the Emperor of the

West, and like a relic of the direct disciple of St. Paul that Dionysius was believed to be, was transported ceremoniously to the French monastery of St. Denys on 8 October 827.[4] Erigena's translation was not only inaccurate; in some cases it said the exact opposite of the original. It was this faulty Latin text, however, which shaped the spirituality of the West for at least two or three centuries.

But it is in his original work, *De Divisione Naturae*, which shows an additional influence of the ideas of Gregory of Nyssa and Maximus the Confessor, whom he also translated, that John Scotus Erigena actually recreated the universe. Etienne Gilson called it an *immense épopée métaphysique*.[5] The same metaphysical construct is expressed in a more lucid way in Erigena's commentary on the Prologue to the Gospel of St. John.

For him, humanity was the center of the universe, though God was its origin:

> Let us remark that the blessed evangelist uses the word 'world' four times (i.e. in John 1:9-10); but he teaches us that there are three worlds, of which the first is absolutely and exclusively constituted of invisible, spiritual powers. To come into this world is to have full participation in the true light. The second is the complete opposite of this world, and is constituted absolutely of visible, corporeal natures. And, though his second world has been placed at the lowest level of the universe, the Logos was in it, and by the Logos was it made. And it is the first level to climb for those who would know the truth through the senses, for it is through recognition of the visible that the rational soul is attracted to the knowledge of the invisible. The third world is that which, as a mediating term, conjoins in itself the superior spiritual world and the inferior corporeal world, and makes the two one. It is only in man, through whom the whole creation is united, that we encounter this third world. Man thus is composed of body and soul. Uniting a body from this world and a soul from the other, he makes of them a cosmos.[6]

Humanity thus harmonizes in itself the visible and the invisible, or, as Maximus said, it is the *syndesmos* or binding thread of the universe,[7] what John Scotus called its *copula*.

John Scotus saw the universe itself as dynamic. Everything is in process, or, to put it more adequately, the universe is a double movement proceeding from and returning to God. But humanity, the kingpin of this universe, has fallen and brought disharmony into the cosmos. God enters the fallen universe in a new way through the incarnation of Jesus Christ whose purpose is to restore the harmony of the universe by restoring human nature. In entering humanity, Christ has entered all; neither nature nor things are excluded from participation in him.

But Erigena could not have conceived of an independent entity called "nature" whether inclusive or exclusive of humanity. The whole of medieval philosophy was never able to make nature into an independent realm. It was always inseparably linked to the "supernatural", from which it arose and by which it was sustained. Moreover, in neither patristics nor the early stages of Western medieval theology does nature as a subhuman aspect of creation receive independent treatment. The judgment of Gilson is worth citing:

> Everywhere in medieval philosophy, the natural order is linked to a supernatural order on which it depends both for its origin and its final destiny. Man is an image of God; the blessedness for which he yearns is a divine blessedness; the only adequate object for his intellect and his will is a transcendent being, before whom his moral life has to be lived out and judged. Further, the physical world itself, created by God for his glory, is operated from within by a sort of blind love which moves it towards its author, and each being, each activity of each being, depends, at every moment, for both its existence and its efficacity, upon an omnipotent will which conserves it. If this is so, can one speak of 'nature' in a Christian philosophy? Or should we not rather say, with Malebranche, that nature is *par excellence* an anti-Christian idea, a remnant from pagan philosophy which has been accepted by imprudent theologians?[8]

But it remains a fact that medieval philosophy has used the concept "nature" in a special way, as something distinct from, though dependent on, what is called the "supernatural". Gilson defines the concept thus:

> In the philosophy of the Middle Ages, as in those of Antiquity, natural entity is an active substance, the essence of which necessarily causes and determines its operations. Nature *(la Nature)*, with a capital N, is nothing but the ensemble of natures; therefore fecundity and necessity remain its attributes.[9]

Nature is thus a realm of necessity. The order of nature is what the natures obey. As John Duns Scotus (with whom Erigena is sometimes confused) said, everything that happens to a being regularly, without the intervention of another cause, arises from the nature of that being. Everything except the human free will works according to inexorable laws, that is, by necessity. All that happens in this world is caused either by the necessity of natures, or by other natures in other worlds making us do things. This idea of nature as necessity is deep-rooted in medieval Roman Catholic theology, and grace, or the supernatural, is the intervention of the divine nature from outside the realm of the natural.

Thomas Aquinas, borrowing from Aristotle, added the element of "chance" to the realm of natural necessity, and somewhat eased its rigidity.[10] Chance, in this conception, has an unintended effect: its causality does not operate according to a chosen goal, but fortuitously. It is like when a coconut falls on a man's head and stuns him — it was not the intention of the coconut or the man, but by chance this was the effect. The element of chance, hazard, the accidental or fortuitous, thus produced holes in the steel sheet of natural necessity. But this element was soon eliminated, for in the late medieval Christian conception everything was either an act of nature, a human act, or an act of God. What appeared to be chance was an act of God, caused by providence, in light of an all-seeing wisdom.

With Thomas Aquinas and Duns Scotus the philosophical position becomes clear and unmistakable. It is God who has willed and effected the existence of a series of secondary causes called natures. His will can change nature as in the miracle of Cana. God is not bound by nature, but nature is bound by the laws given to it by God. So we have two sets of laws, the one subordinate to the other — natural law and divine law (and of course man-made laws which depend on one or the other).

In the case of human nature, the medieval theologians were compelled to admit that not everything was the result of natural necessity. The power of the will to choose actions is part of human nature. While that which operates purely according to necessity has no freedom, and so no personality, no dignity that we need to respect, we humans who have this free will are respected even by God, for he came for our salvation. Human nature is thus superior to other natures.

The beginnings of the objectification and alienation of sub-human reality in medieval Christian philosophy are thus very clear. Though the concept of "nature" as the ensemble of natures occurs infrequently, the beginnings are there. Nature has its own constitution, given to it by God, without any reference to humanity. Humans, like everything else, have a nature, but they can be saved only by grace which comes to them from the supernatural realm. That grace, whose primary function is to remove sin, has of course nothing to do with subhuman nature, which, because it has not sinned, does not stand in need of grace or redemption.

b)   Giordano Bruno's vision of the dynamic universe

When we come to the period of the Renaissance, we find that intrepid Italian philosopher, Giordano Bruno (1548-1600), advocating a dynamic universe akin to that envisioned by the process philosophers of today. In his *De l'Infinito, Universo e Mondi*, published in 1584, he not only postulated an infinite universe and many worlds, but also insisted that the world was throbbing with life and growing towards its own fullness. It is not surprising then that in our time there is a growing interest in Bruno. [11]

Bruno abandoned the medieval world-view along with his Christian faith when he cast off his monk's habit and fled from the Dominican monastery in Naples. He lectured at all the prominent universities of Europe, and was patronized by kings and queens. He could never stick to one place for too long—whether it was the Sorbonne or Oxford, Wittenberg or Vienna. The sources of his thought are to be found in all sorts of mystical and gnostic literature—the *Corpus Hermeticum*, the Jewish *Kabbala*, Henry Cornelius Agrippa's *De Occulta Philosophia*, Lucretius's *De Rerum Natura*, and Sacrobosco's *Tractatus de Sphaera Mundi*, among others.

"God in things" is a recurring phrase in Bruno's writings. The earth itself was for him a living being, as were the sun, which was seen as divine and as controlling life on the earth, the planets, and the stars. Nature was a generating being, full of seminal powers, an image of God, an emanation from him, an ensouled reality through which God is to be known. Here are reflections of Pythagoras and Plato, the Stoics and the Gnostics, and many other systems, eclectically put together.

Bruno revived for Western civilization the cosmos of the Stoics, though, unlike them, he did not box God up within it. He revived the magic and astrology for which the pagan European subconscious thirsted. He may have been a passing phase in the European Renaissance, but he has captured the interest of at least the counter-culturists and is making a comeback as a possible alternative to the single vision of an objectifying, alienating science which treats the world as meat to be carved up according to our tastes and desires.

Yet, in another sense, Bruno's universe appears as the ancestor of that of Newton and Bacon. Expunge the nature of the universe as full of life, and replace the organismic by a mechanistic model; drain the universe of its *anima*, and substitute the control of the laws of inertia and gravity for that of Bruno's capricious planetary forces, and you have the universe of science as it was until yesterday, even after Mach, Minkowski, and Einstein had successfully questioned the mechanical model of Newton and Bacon. Of course, without the empirical knowledge amassed by direct experimentation and the precise work of theoretical physicists and mathematicians, science could not have been brought to birth simply by subtracting the *anima* from Bruno's speculative vision of the universe. But even experimenters and theoretical investigators work with assumptions and conceptions like space, time, matter, energy, and quanta taken from everyday experience. While they may relate these in ingenious ways which help to explain phenomena and predict the behavior of entities, the basic ideas do not spring up in a vacuum: they are compounded of those of which earlier philosophical systems were built.

c) Modern science — only one road to reality

Science today undoubtedly has the possibility of producing a revolution: the theoretical scientists themselves assure us of this. What we already know of microphysics and microbiology has jolted common-sense assumptions. Causality, for example, can no longer be regarded as uniform or homogeneous. A perceptive, but extremely matter-of-fact scientist recognized this almost half a century ago, in the wake of the general acceptance of the theory of relativity and quantum physics:

> The quantum theory suggests that space and time are approximate concepts, which may have to be abandoned when the infinitely small is contemplated. In much the same way, the concept of temperature as due to an agitation of molecules loses its meaning when the molecules themselves are considered.
>
> What the future may hold in store is anyone's guess at the present time. But one thing is certain: we are faced with a gigantic revolution; and the new ideas will undoubtedly conflict with the common-sense instinct which the rationalist often erroneously attributes to 'reason'. [12]

These predictions of Professor Abro have proved increasingly valid, particularly in the field of measurement of quanta at the micro levels. Recent books like *Paradigms and Paradoxes: The Philosophical*

Challenge of the Quantum Domain[13] bring the problems at least in part within the comprehension of the average nonscientist. The notion of "elementary particles" does not correspond with the way the smallest units of matter-energy function. The action of the experimenter seems to be an ineradicable part of reality as known by science, at least at this microlevel. As Heinz Post of the University of London said in a review of the above book,[14] predictive success is no basis for the correctness of the fundamental ontology assumed. The "scandal of quantum mechanics" as the Einstein-Podolski-Rosen paradox is often called, cannot be explained away, as Heinz Post does, by referring it merely to our present theory of measurement, or as Professor Arthur Fine suggests, by asserting "that things are perfectly all right in QM".[15] He argues that certain equations (namely of compounding probability for compound events from the probability of their components) in probability mathematics, which we have previous taken for granted, do not function within the restricted space of the two-slit experiment, and therefore that these equations cannot be regarded as universally true generalizations. What Fine fails to do is to provide an adequate hypothesis for explaining why the consistency with normal probability equations obtains only when the observer-measurer is present and why an inconsistent pattern appears when and only when the measuring-mechanism is not present.

Today, no scientist can deny that a high measure of indeterminacy persists at the micro level of reality. Our laws of probability can function only within limited areas and at certain levels. Science, in discovering this indeterminacy, has now begun to shed its overconfidence about its being able to know all there is to know. The monopoly of knowledge which it previously claimed is today called in question. Yet, scientific research will have to continue, and along with education and culture, it must continue to have sizeable allocations of the taxpayers' money. But science itself has a responsibility to become slightly more sane and perhaps more modest, admitting that its method is only one road to reality, one that reveals significant aspects of reality, but not all aspects of that reality.

2. THE COUNTER-CULTURE ALTERNATIVE

The reaction against the emptiness of a technological civilization produces the strangest results in Western society. There is, for instance, the recourse to Eastern mysticism as the cure-all for the evils

of a technoculture. In Asia, and particularly in India, plenty of manu-
facturers of spiritual commodities are eager to cash in on the new
market, with products like transcendental meditation or *sannyas*
(renunciation) simplified. Instant tranquility in twenty easy lessons
for only a few dollars, and no after-effects!

But there is no call for sarcasm. People who find unbearable the
restlessness produced by urban-technological civilization can achieve
a measure of inner serenity and mental discipline through the practice of daily meditation, using a technique that brings the insights
of Patanjali's yoga system within reach of the ordinary man or woman.
In essence, however, the discipline is not so different from that of daily
morning and evening devotions developed in the Christian tradition.
Hindu meditation may be more attractive to the modern secular
Western mind, mainly because it is exotic and devoid of any dogmatic
assumptions or presuppositions.

But does it go far enough? Does it ask why the urban-technological
civilization makes us so restless? What is it in human nature or in the
nature of reality that accounts for the restlessness? What is the meaning of existence, or what do we live for? These questions are not taken
up at all by the school of transcendental meditation, which states explicitly that it has no intention of dealing with such questions. A Guru
like Maharishi Mahesh Yogi can entertain the most archaic economic
and political ideas, while his technique for personal meditation seems
to be of value to some people.

Zen Buddhism, which is in vogue among many more sophisticated
seekers after tranquility, appears to offer a much more comprehensive
approach to reality, one that denies all validity to conceptual formulations and rational thinking, and is thus diametrically opposed to the
methods and techniques of modern science and technology. Here,
too, one finds only sardonic contempt for all preoccupations with the
social, economic, and political problems which confront us. It seeks
to transcend them by denying their reality. This may "make sense"
to those who have a Zen experience (if Satori can be called experience),
for it is claimed that Zen statements transcend rational categories and
that those without that experience are unable to "make sense" of them.
Our reasons for not accepting Zen as a basis for culture is that it makes
culture itself meaningless.

In the counter-culture syndrome, we find a much more societally-
based world vision. Theodore Roszak[16] is undoubtedly its most articulate prophet. He deserves serious attention, since he speaks to us
from within the occidental culture, and since his criticism of science

and technology is more than a mere emotional reaction. His two books, *The Making of a Counter Culture*[17] and *Where the Wasteland Ends*,[18] have made a profound impression on this writer. His scathing criticism of "Science *in Extremis*: Prospect of an Autopsy" needs a calm response from philosophers of science who hold a different view.

Roszak accuses science of many things: of having "undone the human scale" by routinizing and collectivizing scientific research; of breeding a professional "drone", unimaginative and uninterested in anything but the quantifiable and the technically manageable, an obedient servant of the technocratic society; of dominating and distorting human intellectual effort by imposing the scientific attitude as the only possible attitude for man to assume towards reality; of reducing even the richness of human relations to its predictable aggregate effects; of having brought on the environmental crisis by its unrestricted thirst for knowledge as a means to power; of undoing the open society by creating an elitism of esoteric knowledge; of seeking to undermine political community through quantifying and mechanically manipulating human beings; of assaulting the mysterious character of all reality and reducing everything to "nothing but. . .", thus reducing reality to the flatness of the single vision of which science alone is capable.

His language is lyrical, not academic or scientific. He does not seek to prove; he asserts and affirms and negates with prophetic passion. Roszak makes no claims to be "matter-of-fact" or "down-to-earth". On the contrary, he wants us to move away from our preoccupation with tangible matter and provable facts; he wants the intellect, like an uncaged skylark, to take a rhapsodic flight into the upper spheres, there to soar and roam in the realm of symbols and to experience oneness with the universe in a sentient, full-blooded vision of eternity. Reminds one of Jonathan Livingstone Seagull!

Science is for Roszak the arch-villain. It reduces reality to what it can manage with its own very limited techniques. He cites Abraham Maslow who characterized the reductionist intellect as a "cognitive pathology" usually born of fear, the style of mind which, in the words of Kathleen Raine, wants to make us "see in the pearl nothing but a disease of the oyster". In Roszak's own words:

> Doubtless in our culture, reductionism traces back to the Judaeo-Christian mania for desacralizing nature. It is mixed too with a compulsively masculine drive to demonstrate toughness, to expel sentiment, and to get things under heavy-handed control.[19]

Roszak gives an impressive list of examples of "respectable research by reputable scientists" which seeks the automation of personality, therapy by terror, physical control of the mind, artificial
intelligence and mechanistic counterfeiting of the mind, brain ex-
traction and transplantation, nilhilism in new biology in the style of
Jacques Monod, genetic engineering—all of which he finds destructive
of the genuinely human element in men and women, reducing them
to manipulating subjects or manipulable objects to be homogenized
with lifeless machines and inert objects. Roszak's heroes are Goethe
and Blake, George Fox, Tolstoy and Gandhi, Pathanjali and the Old
Gnostics; his villains Bacon and Descartes, Newton and Saint-Simon,
Christianity and the Rand Corporation.

What then is Roszak's alternative? Where does the wasteland end
and paradise begin? He gives us the blueprint of a "visionary com-
monwealth, a confederated community of communities". His basic
principles are (a) the person first; (b) the community at the grass-roots
and at a worldwide level; (c) the unmaking of the artificial environment and a return to nature; (d) replacing the reductionist intellect
(including the humanist intellect, today in the captivity of single
vision) with a direct vision which does not shy away from the great
metaphysical questions about life and reality.

His own basic orientation becomes evident in the last pages of
Where the Wasteland Ends:

> The higher sanity will find its proper politics when we come to
> realize in our very bones that we have nothing to add to the splendor
> of the old gnosis and can make no progress 'beyond it'. We can do
> no more than return to it, borrow from it, reshape it to suit the
> times. [20]

By the Old Gnosis, Roszak appears to mean, not just historical
gnosticism as we know it, but the ancient and primordial human quest
to see "God in things" and to be united with him in a rhapsodic
experience of eternity in time. Roszak would probably reject the anti-
matter spiritualism of classical gnosticism, though he says very little
about it. It is the return to God that he advocates in very anti-Christian
language— the common way of Bonaventura, Buddha and Lao Tzu.
The apocatastasis that Roszak yearns for is to be triggered by "an illumination in the abyss by which the lost soul, after much tribula-
tion, learns to tell the divine light from its nether reflection". [21] He
restrains his eloquence when he comes to describe this illumination,

for "it is *experience* that must reopen these issues, not academic discourse".

> If there is to be a next politics, it will be a religious politics. Not the religion of the churches — God help us! Not the religion of the churches — but religion in the oldest, most universal sense: which is vision born of transcendent knowledge.[22]

It would be unfair to shoot holes in Roszak's erudite discourse with the guns of our dead logic, for it is against that logic that he wages battle. He selects facts with a ferocious one-sidedness. He distorts science and technology with a mania pardonable only in a prophet. His hatred of Christianity seems to be born of experience, but is uninformed by sufficient acquaintance with its rich tradition. His negativism towards the urban-industrial civilization is unmitigated by the least touch of fairness. Passion takes over and replaces logic in the citadel of the intellect. He is obscure where he seeks to be creative; his alternatives are little more than hunches perilously close to platitudes. But like Giordano Bruno, Theodore Roszak is exciting!

CHAPTER FOUR

Process Theology—An Alternative to the Classical Metaphysics of the West

One theological school in the West claims to have an intellectual alternative to the errors of classical Western metaphysics which brought on the alienation of humanity from nature, and in its wake the eco-crisis. Process theology, therefore, should be listened to with respect. But first we need to consider the American form of process philosophy, in particular the thought of Alfred North Whitehead.

Following our examination of process theology, we shall turn to two other alternatives to classical Western metaphysics: the thinking of Teilhard de Chardin, that extraordinary poet of science and theology whose independent but convergent reasoning is closely related to that of Whitehead and the process theologians, and a classical Christian alternative comparatively unknown in the West—the thought of Gregory of Nyssa.

1. THE WAY OF WHITEHEAD

Alfred North Whitehead was preoccupied with the question of nature in what appears at first to be a disarmingly naïve way. In his essay, *The Concept of Nature*, he begins by stating blandly that natural science is the science of nature,[1] and goes on to ask what nature is. But he does not want an ontological analysis: he is satisfied with a simple answer — that is nature is nothing else than that which gives us sense-knowledge.[2] The primary task of a philosophy of natural science is thus, in purely behavioristic fashion, to elucidate the concept of nature as a complex fact presented to our knowledge, to exhibit the basic entities and their fundmental interrelations in terms of which we can enunciate all the laws of nature, and to make sure that these fundamental entities and relations are adequate to all the relations between entities which occur in nature.[3]

Whitehead tried, at least at this stage of his thought, to divorce philosophy completely from all aesthetic and ethical considerations; he sought a philosophy of the physical universe, one which he expected would provide a conceptual basis for the natural sciences. His intention was more or less the same as that of Edmund Husserl in Germany when he created phenomenology as the science of eidetic or mental essences. Both were seeking an alternative to the Aristotelian metaphysics and logic which saw the universe as composed of material objects in time and space. Both questioned the very idea of matter as a substratum for sense-data. Both held that the static substance-ontology of traditional natural science was based on this erroneous conception of matter as substratum.

Whitehead criticized the traditional substance metaphysics also for separating objects from each other, for seeing them as independent entities rather than as one whole. He was quite concerned about the fissure in nature — the separation between the *experience* of nature and the scientific *conception* of nature, that is the difference between the color of glowing coals as experienced in one's sitting room on a December evening and the scientific explanation of the color red as a particular case of the agitation of molecules. He saw the basic cause of the malady in the fragmentation or splitting up of time, namely, in the conception of time as composed of indivisible static moments, each one passing away and giving place to the next. Time is not a succession of dead moments: it is living duration. Duration is the whole object of our present observation, not just the measure of time during which something static lasts. In Whitehead's thought, time and space are not bifurcated, but are seen as dimensions of the single reality of nature. The whole of nature is composed, not of "things" in something called "time", but of an interconnected series of four-dimensional events — the three spatial dimensions of length, breadth, and thickness, and the dimension of time. "Objects" are not merely characteristics and qualities of an event; they are the characters in the drama of an event.

In this system of events which Whitehead calls nature, reality is no longer seen in the static categories of substance and attributes. Objects are still there, but they no longer exist in pure space; they are parts of events in time-space. Objects are of three categories: sense-objects, objects of perception, and objects of scientific theory. These form an upward moving hierarchy. At the third and highest level— that of scientific formulation—certain fundamental entities and relations in nature have been isolated which are universally valid, and which have meaning only in relation to the two lower levels of mental perception and sense-awareness. They have no significance apart from the whole of nature.

The objects appear and reappear in events. But each event is discreet, unique, is itself and none other. It is Sartre's *l'être en-soi*, being-in-itself. It does not reproduce itself, nor does it change.[4] It has "its own substantial unity of being". But the event is related in significance to the total process of all events in both the past and the future.

Scientific abstractions were for Whitehead an aspect of the reality-event. The electron is abstract for it cannot be isolated from everything else and be made to exist by itself. But so is the smile of a cat abstract, since the smile cannot be separated from the cat. The objects of science are not artificial creations: they are in nature, as the smile of a cat is in the cat-event.

To know nature, through science, is to recognize "scientific objects" in the nature-event which is constantly changing.

Repeatability is a characteristic of scientific objects; they can recur again and again in different events, whereas the event itself is unrepeatable; it is finished, it is past; it has no possibility to recur, as objects do.

An event in nature, when mentally perceived, is an object of the mind. This mental object is adjectivally related to the external object. The external object is experienced only as qualified by the mental object. The latter is a part of nature. Nature is different because of these perception events. The perceiver and the event of perception are also part of nature, not outside of it. Nature without the event of perception cannot be known.

Nature is thus an ensemble of events; each event is related to the ensemble, and has a special significance for the ensemble. Thus each event is related to all other events. The ensemble is nature; each event, as well as the ensemble, has the characteristics of space-time extension and relatedness. Humanity is an integral event in the ensemble. It has special modes of relation both to other events and to the ensemble.

All this of course is an inadequate summary of the early Whitehead, who expressly disavowed any immediate intention to work out a metaphysics of nature. The metaphysics was to be a project for the future. In 1924, he moved from Cambridge, UK, to Cambridge, Mass., USA. In 1925 he published *Science and the Modern World*,[5] where he began to trace the outlines of his metaphysical system, approaching it from the perspective of science. A different approach was provided by his efforts to cope with his own grief at the tragic death of his son, Eric, in World War I. This is reflected in *Religion in the Making*[6] which was published in 1926. The two approaches are then synthesized in the major work, *Process and Reality: An Essay in Cosmology*,[7] which was published in 1929.

Whitehead finds the twin roots of modern science in the classical Greek tradition and in medieval scholasticism. It was the Greek tradition (and not the Judaeo-Christian) that taught us that nature is an ordered whole. Medieval scholastic reasoning trained the Western mind, through centuries of intellectual discipline, in the arduous subtleties of a rigorous logic. Of course, the two together could not by themselves produce modern science. What sparked off the development of modern science was the recourse to direct encounter with nature through the experimental and inductive method pioneered by Bacon and others. But 17th-century science was, in Whitehead's view, too naïve in assuming that the stuff of the universe was simply matter in various configurations scattered through space — a conception in which time was, so to speak, unrelated to matter, and did not enter into its essence. Bergson was also criticizing this kind of time-freezing of the universe in scientific study and the consequent substance metaphysics. Although Whitehead came from an idealist background, and reacted against most idealists,[8] he was at the same time severely critical of the scientific materialism of 17th-century science. He must have related it to the greedy acquisitive materialism of America which was already manifest in the pillaging march to the frontiers that for four centuries constituted the dynamic of the American psyche. But neither Berkeley nor Bradley (who were idealists) had managed to break the power of this materialism in the culture itself.

While fighting the mechanistic-materialistic understanding of nature, Whitehead wanted also to incorporate into his system the valid insights of romantic poets like Wordsworth and Shelley, so that the nature of which they wrote would not be something of more significance than science understands by the concept "nature".

But science itself moved, with the 19th-century discoveries of electromagnetic fields, atomic structure, the theory of conservation of energy, and organic evolution, into viewing nature more as an organism than as a mechanism.[9]

So, in *Process and Reality*, Whitehead starts from certain fundamental, but largely unexamined metaphysical-ontological principles.[10] The "real" world is for him made up of actual "entities" and outside of these entities there is nothing. He attempts to isolate and articulate the necessary conditions for all experience, that is, "to develop all those generic notions adequate for the expression of any possible interconnection of things". The extent to which he succeeds is still to be fully judged.

Whitehead's system is capped by his classic statement on God and the world, which constitutes the concluding chapter of *Process and Reality*. Here he deduces from his empirical thought certain suggestions on thinking about God:

> Viewed as primordial, He is the unlimited conceptual realization of the absolute wealth of potentiality. In this aspect, He is not *before* all creation, but *with* all creation. . . He is the unconditioned actuality of conceptual feeling at the base of things; so that, by reason of this primordial actuality, there is an order in the relevance of eternal objects to the process of creation.[11]

God is for Whitehead the principle of concretion and coherence in the universe. In this sense, God is primordial. But He is also consequent. He is the beginning *and* the end. Beginning, not in the sense of the first of a series, but as originator, as "the presupposed actuality of a conceptual operation". End, not as the final member of the series, but in the sense that every event in the world reacts upon God and constitutes him in his self-objectification as world, which is the mode of God derived from his all-inclusive primordial conceptualizations which is the beginning of the word.

> Thus, analogously to all actual entities, the nature of God is bi-polar. He has a primordial nature and a consequent nature. The consequent nature of God is conscious; and it is the realization of the actual world in the unity of his nature, and through the transformation of his wisdom. The primordial nature is conceptual, the consequent nature is the weaving of God's physical feelings upon his primordial concepts.[12]

Thus, Whiteheadian metaphysics is a bi-polar dialectic consisting of (a) the one infinite primordial conceptual realization of the world in the mind of God; (b) the possibility of multiple finite physical actualizations in the world-process; and (c) the mutual polar identity and unity between the infinite unitary "conceptual feeling" and the finite multiple actualization. Here nature is no longer the simple ensemble of entities that it was in the early Whitehead of the 1920s. Nature is now God's original conceptual feeling, actualizing itself with internal freedom, and the whole constitutes God himself in his actualized self-objectifying phase.

Each temporal occasion, each technological event, is an event in God, and God is in that event. Nature is God in his second pole as the flux of process. God and world are two aspects of the same reality, though contrasting or bi-polar aspects.

> God is the infinite ground of all mentality, the unity of vision seeking physical multiplicity. The world is the multiplicity of finites, actualities seeking a perfected unity. Neither God, nor the world, reaches static completion. Both are in the grip of the ultimate metaphysical ground, the creative advance into novelty. Either of them, God and the world, is the instrument of novelty for the other. . . [13]
>
> The consequent nature of God is the fulfillment of his experience by his reception of the multiple freedom of actuality into the harmony of his own actualization. It is God as really actual, completing the deficiency of his mere conceptual actuality. [14]

We have not attempted here to make a full evaluation of Whitehead, but rather to see the metaphysical import of his own "conceptual feeling". The supple richness and the comprehensive subtlety of the conception are immediately evident. But some questions remain.

a)   The Hindu philosopher would ask: If the cosmos is the actualization of God's conceptual feeling, then was God not unfulfilled and deficient when the cosmos began? Deficiency and consequent desire on the part of God are unthinkable for the classical thinker, whether Hindu or Hellene.

b)   Even though the conceptual pole of God, which is primordial, is conceived as infinite, God seems to become perfect only by adding actuality to the infinitude of his potentiality. The classical thinker would deny that anything can be added to infinity, nor can he conceive of an infinity that is deficient.

THE LIBRARY, UNIVERSITY COLLEGE, GALWAY
INTER LIBRARY LOAN — BOOK APPLICATION

AUTHOR OF BOOK (Block Letters)	BARRETT, M.
TITLE & ANY OTHER DETAILS (Block Letters)	WOMEN'S OPPRESSION TODAY

PLACE OF PUBLICATION	PUBLISHER	EDITION
London	ROUTLEDGE CHPMAN & HALL	
		YEAR
PRICE	SOURCE OF REF.	1988

ISBN NO. 0-860 91-219-1

NAME	ADDRESS
(Block Letters)	Dominic Rh
DEPT.	The Furniner & Neturini—
	Leninism, The Soviet &

TO BE SIGNED ON RECEIPT OF BOOK

PHONE NO. First Grder Experience

DATE Book Review.

I RECEIVED THE ABOVE BOOK AND
UNDERTAKE TO REPLACE LOSS OR DAMAGE.

SIGNED:

DATE:

LATEST DATE FOR USE

Gemma Nicola Power
6 Q St. Pls.
Nicola Power. 10(1):200–201
8

Junginkel, J., Marx u. re. guste of Nohe
→ Book Review
Beitz. Gesch. 27 (4):566-567, 85

Rose, Me.
Turang of Nohe re...
3 Rich Journal of Asians
26(2):150-160, 1986

Levine, R
A Science of Q...Ora — Means — of Nohe
Mon Rev
Monthly Review in... 38(3):3-12, 1986

Best myp Zur Geschichte Der
Arbeiterbewegung

APPLIED	RECEIVED	DUE	RETURNED

RENEWAL APPLIED FOR — RENEWED

c)   Novelty, or creative novelty, which Whitehead conceives to be his fundamental metaphysical principle motivating even the purpose of God, is after all a time concept. Can one reverently ask whether God was bored before the creation began? By making time-space extension a necessary aspect of God's very being, by moving so easily from the mode of existence of created beings to the being of the creator, are we not carrying the principle of analogy too far? According to the traditional Christian position, time, experienced as the inevitability of death, is experienced exclusively by beings who have been created out of nothing and will return to nonbeing. For God, time in its entire duration is copresent, and is not something to be traversed from beginning to end. Whitehead seems too easily to project on to God human time-experience.

d)   A traditional Christian like the present writer, who refuses to accept some of the misinformed charges against traditional Christianity—for example, that it has a static view of God or of the universe —would recognize that Whitehead has made a rather lucid and interesting exposition of the classical Christian view of the universe, but that he has too simply and unqualifiedly identified the Logos immanent in the world with the creator. A more sophisticated trinitarian-incarnational doctrine, while assimilating much of Whitehead's doctrine of God, would avoid that simple identification.

The most vulnerable point in any philosophy is its assumptions, the basic intuitions which it does not set out to demonstrate, but which nevertheless in some sense constitute both the method used and the conclusions arrived at. As William Ernest Hocking said of Whitehead's metaphysics:

> A descriptive metaphysics does not come forward with a proof of its case: but it has its assumptions which constitute starting points. The philosopher's good faith consists in announcing the assumptions he makes—when he is aware of them. And since they occupy the paradoxical position of initial finalities, such assumptions should be 'intuitions' in the sense of what one 'sees' to be true with sufficient assurance to put it forward as premises. They are points of accepted vulnerability.
> Whitehead is peculiarly liberal in these assumptions, and although it belongs to his bent to choose them in wholly personal fashion, he commonly puts them forward as deliverances of common sense, positions which it would be a bit foolish not to take for granted.[15]

Hocking then goes on to provide a sample list of seven of these assumptions which carry "the main load of [Whitehead's] argument":

a) reality is becoming;
b) no primary substances;
c) flux realizes "eternal entities";
d) togetherness is never an external relation;
e) perception deals with the actual, not with representations of the actual;
f) action intends to affect real being outside myself;
g) there is no All-One.

This is not the place to examine what may be some of the assumptions underlying Whitehead's metaphysics. But they must be recognized as assumptions, not as scientifically-demonstrated truths.

2. PROCESS IN THEOLOGY

Process theology, based on Whitehead's process philosophy, is advanced as a healthier theological vision of the humanity-nature relation than traditional Western theology. John Cobb, for example, finds it the only viable alternative to the heavily man-centered Judaeo-Christian view, which, in ascribing absolute value to the individual, reduces the value of the rest of creation to its mere usefulness for humankind.[16]

Traditional Christian theology, Cobb charges, has been essentially "exclusivist", that is to say, it has seen man as the sole object of God's concern, and therefore excluded the subhuman world from the pale of salvation. Theology sees humanity as something totally different from the rest of creation. According to Cobb, this exclusivist stance can be traced back to Descartes who "began by separating man metaphysically from all else in a way more drastic than had ever been done in western philosophy".[17]

It cannot be denied that Descartes saw the world in a somewhat static way, as composed of *things*, objects of perception. But the reality status of these objects was questioned in the ensuing epistemological debate in the West. We had access only to the sense-data in ourselves, not to the object as such or in itself. Kant completed what Descartes began. For him, the world was a product of the interaction of sense-data and categories supplied by the structure of the human mind. Western philosophy thus became preoccupied with the mind, since things-in-themselves exist only in the form of presence in the human mind.

Process philosophy's great contribution, according to Cobb, comes at two points. First, it conceives of the world as composed of events in time rather than of things in space. Second, it shifts the focus of preoccupation away from the workings of the human mind to the continuous universe in which man is a participant and not necessarily the dominant master of the all-important center. Cobb calls Whitehead the father of an "ecological philosophy". By showing that the ultimate components of even those articles which we regard as objects are in fact electro-magnetic events, Whitehead undercut the neat distinction between nature and history, a distinction so dear to many Western intellectuals.

Process theology, a child of traditional neo-Calvinism and Whiteheadian philosophy, is a self-conscious American youngster clamoring for attention and not always getting it. One of its more eloquent contemporary spokesmen, Schubert Ogden, makes the claim this way:

> Among the most significant intellectual achievements of the 20th century has been the creation at least of a neoclassical alternative to the metaphysics and philosophy theology of our classical tradition. Especially through the work of Alfred North Whitehead and . . .Charles Hartshorne, the ancient problems of philosophy have received a new, thoroughly modern treatment, which in its scope and depth easily rivals the so-called *philosophia perennis*.[18]

For Whitehead's own metaphysical construction, Ogden simply refers us to *Process and Reality*.[19] The cornerstone of the system of process philosophy is the movement away from the *secondary* phenomenon of the world, which according to Ogden occupied the center of classical philosophy, to the "reformed subjectivist principle" of the *primal* phenomenon of selfhood.

Ogden contends that an acceptable doctrine of God can be constructed on the analogy of the self as a relational center rather than as substance. The self is the sum total of the events in which it has participated up to any given moment, and is continuously in a process of relating itself to other events and being formed and reformed in the course of these relations.

> I know myself most immediately only as an ever-changing sequence
> of experience, each of which is the present integration of remembered
> past and anticipated future into a new whole of significance.[20]

It is on this analogy that Ogden constructs his notion of God:

> God is by analogy a living and even growing God and . . . He is
> related to the universe of other beings somewhat as the human self
> is related to its body.[21]

From this, it is clear why Whiteheadian philosophy has been
called an "ecological philosophy", for it seems made to order to help
us face the problems of alienation between God, humanity, and the
world: all three are put in one inclusive package, and there need be
no alienation.

Among the charges usually made against process theology is that
it smacks of pantheism. Ogden responds that it is more like pan-en-
theism, that is, the doctrine that everything is in God, rather than
that everything *is* God. The charge is usually made by those who conceive of God as someone distinct from the world. Ogden is right,
within the limits of his own knowledge, when he says:

> Either one must conceive of God with Aquinas as wholly external
> to the world, something merely alongside it, and so but part of a
> whole somehow including God and the world together; or else one
> must say with Spinoza that it is God who includes the world, but
> only so as to make the world itself wholly necessary and our experi-
> ence of its contingency and dependence an illusion.[22]

Another criticism is that the God of process theology is not quite
perfect and has to become something other than He now is. Process
philosophy would respond that growth does not mean the absence
of perfection, nor does the absence of growth mean perfection. God
is perfect at every moment of his being, in that his "unsurpassability
by others is a matter of principle, not simply of fact".[23]

While, as we stated earlier, there remain certain questions which
process theologians have yet to answer adequately, they do face square-
ly the question of transcendence. They claim that it is naive to conceive
of God's transcendence in spatial terms since this, by making the
cosmos other than God, makes God less than the whole package God-
world. The transcendence of God is temporal, that is, in terms of the

future. He is always moving beyond to the future and therefore cannot be enclosed by space plus past time.

In this perspective, the future of humanity is but part of the future of the universe, which in fact is the future of God. The three are integrally related—with the important qualification that even if the earth and sea and all that are in them were to perish and evaporate into total non-being, God would survive, insofar as the rest of the universe went on. God's being, though changed by the destruction of the earth and of the whole biosphere-noösphere in it, would continue through other beings, processes, and events in other parts of the universe.

In this context, it is true that, though the future of humanity is theoretically separate from that of God, for the Christian who believes that God has become man in Christ, the future of God has become the future of humanity. It is in this sense that Fr. Edward Schillebeeckx's *God, the Future of Man*,[24] is understood, though at this point he may be more indebted to Teilhard de Chardin than to Whitehead.

3. TEILHARD DE CHARDIN:
COSMOGENESIS AND HOMINIZATION

Permanence-change, staticity-flux, inertness-consciousness, transcendence-immanence: these polarities seem perennially to pose problems for any metaphysics. Whitehead seizes on the problem of permanence-change and tries to reveal its double dimension. His whole metaphysics is based on this fundamental dualism between, on the one hand, a God who has to complete his own "primordial" being by continually and permanently deriving his "consequent" being from the flux of the temporal world, and, on the other, an actually flowing world needing to find permanence through its actuality being absorbed by the permanent God and eternalized in the very being of God.

Teilhard de Chardin, coming out of palaeontology, biology, and theology, takes a different track to get at the same problem. He does not seek to build a metaphysical system, but enquires deeply into the structure of the universe. Unlike Whitehead, Teilhard finds no difficulty in acknowledging the great gaps that exist in our knowledge. While Whitehead manifests the theologically unsophisticated scientist's assurance that he possesses all the necesssary tools for exploring reality, and tries to construct a fully adequate system of knowledge, Teilhard, with proper Christian modesty, recognizes that the gaps in our knowledge are inherent in the very structure of the universe. "Direct perception of the origins of anything is automatically denied to our eyes as soon as a sufficient depth of the past is interposed."[25]

Teilhard sees the universe as in a process of continuous evolution, and believes that it is not possible correctly to appreciate the human "position in the world without first determining the place of life in the universe".[26] He therefore seeks to build a bridge between physics and biology, that is to say, between the physical universe and all of life. He psychoanalyzes the hesitation of modern science to accept the nature of life as a way of understanding the physical universe, and its insistence on using the laws of physics and chemistry to understand life. According to Teilhard, the basic structure of the universe is revealed more clearly in the field of biology and of human development than in the much more primitive or simple laws of the physical universe. Life is not an epi-phenomenon of matter, nor is thought simply an epi-phenomenon of life. It is the higher phenomena that manifest to us the true nature of fundamental reality.

Life is the central phenomenon of reality, "the very essence of phenomenon".[27] Life is the flower of the universal phenomenon of matter in process of evolution through a basic pattern of increasing complexity-centricity. If the elements that compose the universe are plotted graphically according to their complexity-intensity, the graph curve shoots up from particle to virus to animal to man. It then levels off: man is the most complexly-organized part of the known universe, and evolution in the form of increasing complexity-centricity seems to have come to its pinnacle in humankind.

This is a quite different parameter from those we use to evaluate things, such as size. In the past, we have seen the elements of the universe as ranging in size from atoms to stars, and saw man as rather insignificant in the vastness of universal space. But when we use the parameter of intensity-complexity, we see that the vast galaxies of the star-studded universe are not half as complex as the human brain, and that man, despite his insignificant size compared to the macrocosmos, is the most "advanced" or "perfected" organism known to science. Infinity is not to be seen in terms of the infinitely small or the infinitely large, or even as number: infinity is better understood as the constantly-receding horizon of complexity-centricity.

Life is not an accident in the universe. Man is not an absurdity thrown up by the march of the atoms; he is the most advanced point in the purposive evolution of the universe. The emergence of life (vitalization or phyletization) and the emergence of humanity (manifestation of the noösphere, or hominization) are the two great events in the history of the universe. But these transition events still remain closed to our knowledge. Teilhard thinks this is in the very nature of things:

> Just as with any other living form, we must realize that the very earliest human origins, from their very nature and however much we magnify the little we can get hold of, can never be the object of direct experiential knowledge.[28]

While the origin of man remains obscure, we know that the specific group *homo sapiens*, in the early period after its emergence, behaved in much the same way as every other zoological phylum as it shoots into existence. Humanity is just as much a product of the process of evolution as the rest of nature. But as the phylum of man moved into adolescence, it manifested some new characteristics: (a) an extraordinary power of expansion over the face of the earth; (b) extreme rapidity of differentiation of types; (c) a surprising persistence of phyletic germinative power, and (d) an unusual capacity for interconnection between branches with a single fascicle.[29] Socialization, or association in symbiosis through psychic interconnections of histologically independent and strongly individuated units of corpuscles, is only the continuation and replication of the fundamental process that guides evolution — increasing complexity-centricity.

Physical universe, nature, life, socio-politico-economic organization — all these belong to the same basic movement of the cosmos, and humanity is part of that movement, not outside of it.

> From this point of view, the formation of tribes, nations, empires, and finally of the modern state, is simply a prolongation. . .of the mechanism which produced animal species.[30]

The idea of human individuality, that is, that each "person" can achieve fulfillment by seeking his own fulfillment, is a mirage, a delusion, according to Teilhard. The social environment is not something provided to enable each individual to attain his own personal fulfillment. On the contrary, it is the pressure of socialization which teaches us that the true fulfillment of the individual occurs when society itself finds fulfillment. The population pressure, urban congestion, the technology that breaks through space and time as barriers to communication and creates one compressed humanity—all these are forcing the human gas molecules in the glass jar of the earth to undergo a subtle transformation. The compression of vitalized matter leads to a new response in a new organization. Humanity, regarded as a single organism, is being compressed. Our resource depletion and population explosion are simply signs that the pressures are leading us to a new planet-wide reorganization of humanity in a new pattern of greater intensity-complexity.

> . . .the planetization we so dread is simply, to judge from its effects, the authentic direct continuation of the evolutionary process from which, historically, the human zoological group emerged.[31]

Teilhard would say that this is not time for us to lose our nerve about science and technology. The pain we experience is a growing pain:

> In fact, if we watch what we are doing, we shall find in the current of totalization that at present seems to be trying to snatch us away from ourselves and de-centre us, simply a fresh beginning—still the same, but on a higher plane—of the process of corpusculization that generates life. After appearing to have reached its zenith in producing the seed of reflective consciousness, this same process is now setting about grouping together and synthesizing these seeds of thought. After man, we get mankind.[32]

If it is cosmogenesis that is going on, if the period of colonial expansion and aggressive science-technology marked the movement of expansion-totalization, then we are now seeing a turn of the cosmic curve towards complexity-centricity which must then lead to a better corpuscular organization of the organism called humanity. Science and technology must not simply sit in the wings wringing their hands about all the damage done, but shift gears and move into a new phase.

In fact, Teilhard holds the view that eventually it is human research that must show the way out. Research is the groping of the species to find its way—a characteristic act of all phyla in the stream of evolution. Research is thus "one of the fundamental properties of living matter",[33] "necessarily as old as the awakening of thought on earth".[34] But research has received tremendous new impetus in the last couple of centuries because of the development of science and technology. Teilhard thinks we are now in the "Age of Research",[35] and that the research explosion is among the many exponentially increasing entities. This is a sign that evolution is making a new start.

> It is not by chance that the number of research students and their interconnections are increasing 'exponentially' within a mankind that is in process of concentration upon itself.[36]

Teilhard works out in detail the analogy between the way the law of corpuscular expansion-concentration operates everywhere in the evolving universe, and the way in which humanity has been moving from individuation to reorganization in greater centered complexity. Humanity, as a biological organism integrally within nature, is getting ready for a concerted effort to discover where it has to move next, and then to leap to that next stage of transcendence. It must not only make optimum use of the science-technology available to it, but also in its forward movement carry the rest of nature with it, for in transcending himself man does not separate himself from the stream of evolution of which he is the spearhead and captain.

This "entry into convergence" of humanity implies not only pain, but also risk. The facts do not offer any guarantee that the effort is going to be successful. It may be abortive. "Life is less certain than death." The experiment of evolution will be successful only if the necessary external and internal conditions exist. Here it is best to quote Teilhard himself at some length, for what he wrote five years before his death has today become dramatically relevant.

> First, *the external conditions.* By these I mean primarily the manifold reserves (of time, of material, both nutritional and human), that are essential to keep us supplied until the operation is complete. Should the planet become uninhabitable before mankind has reached maturity; should there be a premature lack of bread or essential metals; or, what would be still more serious, an insufficiency, either in quantity or quality, of cerebral matter needed to store, transmit, and increase the sum total of knowledge and aspirations that at any given moment make up the collective germ of the noösphere; should any of these conditions occur, then there can be no doubt that it would mean the failure of life on earth; and the world's effort fully to centre upon itself could only be attempted again elsewhere at some other point in the heavens.
>
> Next, *the internal conditions,* by which I mean those bound

up with the functioning of our liberty. First, a *know-how to do*, sufficiently expert to avoid the various traps and blind alleys (politico-social mechanization, administrative bottlenecks, over-population, counter-selections), so frequently to be met on the road followed by a vast whole in process of totalization. Secondly, and most important of all, a *will to do*, strong enough not to retreat before any tedium, any discouragement, or any fear met on the road.[37]

Together Whitehead and Teilhard constitute important landmarks in recent Western thought. They deserve much closer attention than they have so far received. Teilhard's inclusive view of humanity and nature needs to be placed within the context of the trinitarian economy of creation-redemption. And it is at this point that the classical Christian cosmology of Gregory of Nyssa becomes extremely interesting and relevant.

God's Activity in the World — Gregory of Nyssa and the Classical Christian Alternative

In this chapter, we shall attempt to describe the relationship of God, universe, and humanity as seen by Gregory of Nyssa whose thought in a sense laid the foundations for the classical Christian understanding of the cosmos, though it seems never to have really penetrated the Western Christian tradition.

St. Gregory of Nyssa's reflection on the nature of creation was inspired by the insights of his older brother, St. Basil, who had emphasized the syngenous character of heaven and earth, of eternity and time. St. Basil's nine homilies on the six days (*Hexaemeron*)[1] of creation — an extended commentary on Genesis 1:1-26 — demonstrate his boldness in stating that heaven and earth have come to be by the same divine action and are worthy of equal honor. St. Basil, however, did not develop the concept of time and space in a philosophically-consistent manner, and it was left to St. Gregory of Nyssa to elaborate his brother's thought in a more coherent way.

As Gregory of Nyssa reflects on the nature of the world and of human existence, he does not claim to be doing "theology"; he simply attempts to reflect in faith on God's activity in us and in our environment. In our day, when "theologies of..." are beginning to proliferate, it may be helpful to remember that he, like the other Cappadocian fathers, tries to be as precise as possible in the application of the term "theology". The Cappadocians distinguish two possibilities for reflection—on *theologia* and on *oikonomia*. The first is to correct errors in statements about the trinitarian mystery of God. The second is to reflect on the way God runs the universe, the central fact of that house-management or divine economy being the incarnation, birth, life, death, resurrection, ascension, and continuing activity of the second person of the Trinity. The Cappadocians apply the term "theology" only to the former, that is, strictly to the statements about the triune God, and insist on limiting discussion about theology to the minimum possible, for further intellectual effort is likely to yield little further understanding of the incomprehensible divine nature.

We shall attempt only to point to some of the central aspects of the thought of Gregory of Nyssa within the context of our theme, and not try to do justice to the full richness of the intricate theological system of this 4th-century thinker who sought to integrate the best of contemporary pagan knowledge by using the authentic Christian tradition as the criterion for accepting or rejecting the insights of Greek, Egyptian, and Chaldean thinkers.

1. THE DUALITY OF REALITY

Many students of Gregory of Nyssa have sought to interpret his basic cosmology as Platonic, that is, a view of the universe as composed of two parts: the world of forms—united, transcendent, intelligible, nontemporal, and the world of particulars—multiple, evanescent, sensible, temporal. It is clear that Gregory did know Plato and used many of his categories, figures, and arguments. But it is inadequate to equate Gregorian with Platonic cosmology.[2]

There is a fundamental distinction between Plato, on the one hand, and the Stoics and Aristotle, on the other. The latter are cosmological monists, that is to say, for them the cosmos is one single reality which is limited to what can be known through the senses. There is no region of permanent, unchanging reality. But for Plato, the sensible world is only a ladder by which one ascends to the intelligible world. In his *Republic*,[3] he has Socrates say that the purpose of the true study of mathematics and astronomy is to discern the patterns in the sensible universe which can lead us to the contemplation of the intelligible super-cosmos. This is also the point of the *Phaedrus* myth. In his *Timaeus*, we find again the dual scheme—the eternal world and the temporal world, the ancestor perhaps of the Judaeo-Christian concept of heaven and earth.[4] For Plato, the sensible world is God, not in an ultimate sense, but in a derived or secondary one. It is a *theos aisthetos*, a God open to the senses, a *deuteros theos*, a second God.

Plato thus seems in some way to identify the intelligible world with (the first) God: otherwise how can he see the universe as the second? At first glance, this seems to be quite the opposite of Stoic monism which holds to a strict matter-oriented theology. For a Stoic, God is primordial, the soul, the whole of the cosmos, who does not need to be found *beyond* the universe. Stoicism, however, cannot be called strict monism, for though God is in and inseparable from the universe, He is not merely its sensible elements, but rather the conceptual order which regulates and animates it. While Plato, too, accepts the idea of the the universe as "en-souled", there is a distinction between the dualism of Plato and that of the Stoics.

We could say, with Joseph Moreau,[5] that Platonic dualism is dialectical, transcendent, and teleological, while Stoic dualism is hylozoic, that is, matter and spirit are united in the cosmos as body and soul. The Stoics are basically empiricists: we have to make sense of what we know through our senses. God is the seminal Logos of the universe — and that is *all* either He or the Logos is. The universe is a living being — God. The sensible elements in it are the body of God. He is the generative power which gives rise to the various changing forms which come to be and then pass away. But the whole is eternal, unperishable.[6] In a way, this Stoic concept is the ancestor of the concept of "nature" in deistic and post-Renaissance thinking.

Cherniss shows how Gregory rejects this hylozoistic monism of the Stoics, and then goes on to identify Gregory's view with that of Plato. While it is true that Plato does say that the physical or sensible universe is a state through which we have to pass in order to reach the truly permanent world into which sensation does not enter,[7] the complete identification is too facile. Although Gregory's debt to Plato cannot be denied, the full grandeur of his conception is revealed only in the perspective of the whole structure of his thought, which is quite different from that of Plato.

2. THE CREATOR AND THE CREATION

a) The infinity of God

Ekkehard Mühlenberg, a perceptive Protestant student of Gregory of Nyssa, has advanced the thesis that he was the first Christian thinker to go beyond Plato and Aristotle to introduce into theology the concept of the infinitude of God and to work out all its consequences.[8] But the infinitude which he posited is completely different from the *apeiron* (boundlessness) in the thought of Plato and Aristotle. Plato's definition was rudimentary:

> The One therefore is infinite, since it has neither beginning nor end.[9]

Aristotle, in the *Physics*, after the usual criticism of all previous opinions on the subject, gives his novel definition of infinity:

> Not that outside which nothing exists, but that outside which something more always exists — that is infinity.[10]

The definition is facetious, for if Aristotle really thought that the unbounded has no boundaries, in what sense could he speak of *exo*, outside? The only way to make sense of it is to think of the "outside" as applying to our thought and not to the universe itself. In other words, however far we may go in thought, we shall never reach the boundary. The conceptual bounds within which we try to enclose God can never hold him.

For Plato, and perhaps also for the more Platonic of the Alexandrian fathers like Clement or Origen, the distinctiveness of God's infinity lies in its simplicity and indivisibility. For Gregory, the distinctive element is his "nonfinite" character (*apeiron*), which makes him undefinable (*aoriston*), ineffable (*aphraston*), and incomprehensible (*aperilepton*). In drawing our attention to this fact, Mühlenberg sought to correct the long-standing misinterpretation of Gregory in exclusively mystical terms, so characteristic of great Western Gregorian scholars like Daniélou and Völker, and to a certain extent Balthasar and Jaeger.

Gregory's central notion of the infinity of God has enormous consequences for our understanding of humanity and the whole cosmic process. He has the intellectual courage to say that humanity, and even the cosmos itself, participates in this infinity, though he maintains a radical distinction between uncreated infinity and participated eternity. God is thus not simply someone at the top of the hierarchy of perfections. Indeed, the idea of perfection itself makes sense only if it is freed from any finite limits and made dynamic rather than static. Gregory's view of the perfection of man or the universe was not static. He saw it rather as *infinite advance in the good*, as a never-ending *process*.

An even more sophisticated element in Gregory's thought is that the very notion of "infinity" has little to do with God's *ultimate nature*, since after all, infinity, or boundlessness, is a negative concept drawn from our own experience of finitude. He therefore does not propose God's infinity as the only central category, and rather tries to show the pitfalls in any intellectual enterprise which seeks to move too easily to the infinity of God on the basis of categories and models drawn from finite existence.

b) Ousia and energeia

The distinction between God's being and his operation, so central to Gregory of Nyssa's understanding of the God-world relationship, grew on him during his controversy with the anhomoian or unitarian Cappadocian, Eunomius, for whom it was a pragmatic epistemological principle. According to the latter, each *ousia* or *being* can be understood only through its works or *erga*. The *erga* are effected by the activity or operation or *energeia* of the being (*ousia*). Particular *energeia* or operations always effect the same *erga* or works; differences in works are a consequence of differences in operations. And differences in operations are grounded in differences in beings. So the epistemological principle is: study the *erga* in order to understand the *energeia* which produced it, and thus the *ousia* to which the *energeia* belongs or is attached.

Gregory, in refuting this principle, points out how inadequate it is to understand the *ousia* of the wind from its *ergon* which may be a sand dune. How do you understand the *ousia* of a man who builds both a ship and a house by examining one or the other? By which of its *erga* can we understand the *ousia* of the sky? In the same way, how can the being of God be comprehended through his operations? Gregory denies Eunomius's conception that the *energeia* of God is extremely important for the understanding of the nature of the universe and the human relation to it.

Gregory insists that the *ousia* of God remains inaccessible to us, both intellectually and ontologically. He follows his brother, Basil, who held that at best we could have only an indistinct and vague notion of God's power and wisdom. However, when our lives are cleansed of evil, we can know God, both through his activity, his *energeia*, which is everywhere in the universe, and by understanding ourselves as we gradually become more conformed to his image. But the enterprise of knowing God's *ousia* through his activity is, according to Gregory, a perilous one:

> For how can our understanding, traversing the diastematic (i.e. space-time) extension, comprehend the unextended nature? The enquiry, proceeding through temporal sequence by analysis, goes on to the antecedents of that which has been discovered. Even if diligent research were to traverse all that is known, it would discover no mechanism by which to traverse the very conception of time (*aion*) itself, being unable to stand outside of itself and to surpass time which is the presupposition for all existents... So when language (reason or discourse, i.e. *Logos*) arrives at that which is beyond language, it is time to be silent (Eccles. 3:7), and to marvel at the wonder of this ineffable power, uninterpreted and forbidden to the understanding, realizing that it was only of the works of God and not of God himself that even the great ones (prophets) spoke: 'Who shall declare the powers of the Lord?' (Ps. 105:2), and 'I will narrate all thy works' (Ps. 9:2 or Ps. 117:19) and 'Generations and generations shall praise thy works' (Ps. 144:4). Of these works they speak and of these they relate the details; to declare events which have happened they lend their voices. But when discourse comes to that which concerns him who is above all conception, they prescribe utter silence. For they say: 'For the majesty of the glory of his holiness there is no limit' (Ps. 144:1-5). Ah! How marvellous! How the discourse fears to approach the vicinity of the knowledge of God's nature! So much so, that it does not seek to comprehend even some of the external phenomena that we can apprehend about God. For the text does not say: 'The *ousia of God has no limits*', *judging it too presumptuous to make even such a statement about the concept (of the ousia* of God), but devotes the discourse merely to marvelling at the magnificence in the glory that is seen around God. But even there, the discourse does not take pleasure in seeing even the glory of the *ousia* itself: it is astounded merely by apprehending the *holiness* of that glory. It not only totally abandons every attempt to circumscribe the divine nature and to say what it is; it does not even presume to express wonder at the outermost of its manifestations. For the writer marvels neither at the holiness of God, nor at the glory of that holiness, but only at the *majesty* of the holiness of that glory, and even there he is seized by wonder. The understanding could not grasp even that admirable majesty, for it has no limit! So he says: 'For the majesty of the holiness of his glory there is no limit!' So in discoursing about God, whenever the inquiry turns to the *ousia*, that is 'a time for silence', but when it concerns any of the operations of the good, the knowledge of which comes down even to us, then it is time to speak, to use words, to speak of the powers, to declare the marvels, to narrate the works.[11]

As God's *ousia*, his being, his *is-ness*, remains inaccessible to our concepts or words, it is only of his creation, the derived being of the cosmos, that we can have partial conceptual knowledge. While, thanks to science, this knowledge is constantly increasing, it would be foolish to presume that it will ever be exhaustive. There is no philosophical or theological justification for science's easy optimism of yesterday that, because phenomenal reality is in principle knowable, it is knowable in its entirety. Every generation has to create its own vision of reality and shape its life in accordance with it. We have neither the responsibility, nor the possibility, to know the whole of reality before we begin to shape our lives. In fact, according to Gregory, ever new aspects of reality will manifest themselves to us as our lives become increasingly conformed to the "image", that is, to the good.

3. CONTINUITY–DISCONTINUITY

a)   Diastema and metousia

The basic cosmological question—the problem that has preoccupied the thinkers and seers of all ages and cultures—is that of continuity/discontinuity between God and the universe. We cannot enter here into an extended discussion of the human cosmologies characteristic of different cultures and languages. There are so many variations seen within a single culture that any easy generalization is impossible. We shall, however, venture one generalization, knowing that there are important exceptions to it: Indo-Hellenic cosmology emphasizes continuity between God and the world, while Semitic cosmology puts the emphasis on the discontinuity. The Reformed tradition of Christianity basically follows the Semitic pattern in its exposition of the doctrines of the transcendence of God and the creation of the Universe.[12]

Hellenistic philosophy was always preoccupied with the recalcitrant dualism in all theism, that is, if the One and the Many are different, then there are two realities. The Gnostics and later the Manicheans accepted this dualism and began to influence Christian thought. Two eternal principles—God and the universe, spirit and matter, good and evil, light and darkness— seem to recur in most Hellenistic systems. Stoicism sought to overcome this dualism by making God the soul of the universe. But the body-soul dualism remained.

Neoplatonism then attempted to resolve the difficulty by the notion of the "chain of being", borrowed from the earlier tradition; and this reconciliation was operative in the "grand enemies of the Gospel" like Arius, Aetius and Eunomius against whom Gregory contended.

Gregory was aware of how Origen, Plotinus's contemporary, and the source of many of Eunomius's and Gregory's own ideas, had sought to solve the problem by positing the coeternity of the Son and the Father, the former being the will and wisdom of the latter and as such always present with him. But this meant for Origen, as Gregory saw, that the creation that subsists in the Son was also always with the Father, and as such eternal. Therefore God could not have changed from a God-without-creation to a God-with-creation. As Father Florovsky points out in a very perceptive article on the creation in St. Athanasius, the key word *Pantokrator*, which the Nicene Creed used for God, means ruler-over-all, and this traditional term was understood by Origen to mean that the *ta panta* (the all), or the universe over which God is *Pantokrator*, must have eternally coexisted with him.[13] But it was precisely this notion that made it easy for the early Arians to bracket the Son with the creation, and for Eunomius to seek a compromise in seeing the Son as unique, because begotten by the *energeia* of the Father, yet still part of God's other dimensions. Athanasius tried to break the Origenian knot by boldly proposing a gap between the absolute, self-generating being of God and the dependent, derived, contingent being of the creation. He put the Son and the Spirit on the God-side of the cleavage, since the Son was not the product of God's will but his very hypostasis.[14]

This Athanasian concept of a hiatus or cleavage serves a fundamental function in Gregory's cosmology. He uses as a philosophical term the Greek word *diastema*, which, in Classical Greek, was used in geometry for the distance between two points, in music for the interval between two notes on a scale, and in astronomy for the distance between two celestial bodies. Etymologically, it means "standing apart". In the Arian controversy, the heretics used it to denote the time interval between the origin of the Father and the origin of the Son, "*then* when the Son was not". The orthodox point in the controversy was that no such interval can be posited in relation to the trinitarian God-head, because the God-head has no "extent". Gregory took the idea a stage further, defining *diastema* or extension in space-time in a threefold sense:

    i)   negatively, there is no *diastema* or space-time extension in the being of God, which has no beginning or end, boundary or parts;

    ii)   positively, everything in creation has *diastema* or space-time extension, since space and time are bounded, divisible, with a beginning, an end, and an interval in between;

    iii)   postively-negatively, there is a *diastema*, strictly one-way, between the being of the creation and the being of the creator. There is no way, conceptually or ontologically, to pass from the *ousia* of the creation to the *ousia* of the creator. In the other direction, that is, from the creator to the creation, there is no *diastema*, since the whole of creation from beginning to end and from boundary to boundary is permanently copresent with the creator.[15]

Gregory deals with the problem of dualism in a novel way, though the effort remains incomplete. To the pole of *diastema* which posits one-day discontinuity between God and the universe, he opposed the pole of *metousia* or participation in the *energeia* of God. Plato had used the term *metousia* to speak of the being of particular existents as a participation of an idea. While Gregory does not apply the Platonic notion of the world of ideas, he does define participation as the decisive principle of existence for all creation.[16] Having first emphasized the full transcendence of the One, he can now point out that all levels of reality are dependent, not on each other, but on the single reality of the *energeia* of God. Humanity and nature (the sub-human aspect of the visible creation), as well as the invisible world of angels and powers, are all equally dependent on the *energeia* of God, both for their coming into being and for their continued existence.

b)   Created existence as participation

Plotinus, basing himself on a sentence of doubtful meaning in Plato,[17] but conceivably under the strong influence of Indian thought, denied all reality to matter, reducing it to nonbeing. For him, matter was neither soul nor *nous*, neither power nor receptacle, but a mere reflector of qualities and unaffected by them, undetermined, undefined, and with "no title to the name of being. . . more plausibly called a non-being".[18] For Neoplatonism, matter is a phantasm within a phantasm, a lie, a trickery, incapable of change, indestructible, persistent, like a bad dream that will not go away. It cannot participate in being, and only seems to participate in form. Being is essentially good; matter is essentially evil.

It is this view which Gregory resolutely refutes on the basis of a Christian doctrine of creation. When human beings create, they first form ideas in their minds, then look for the material with which to realize these forms, and then go to work to shape them. The process of God's creation, however, cannot be understood on the analogy of human creation. In him, there is no sequence of will, wisdom, and operation, for sequence belongs only to time-existence. God's will, wisdom, and the effective completion of what He knows and wills all take place instantaneously with no time-interval between them. In his homily on the *Hexaemeron*, Gregory states this explicitly:

> In the divine nature, effective power is concurrent (*syndromos*) with the decreeing will, and the will becomes the measure of the power of God (i.e. in each existent), for the will is wisdom. And the specific characteristic of wisdom is never to be ignorant of how each thing comes to be. So the effective power operates simultaneously with the knowledge. In God's knowledge of the existents was concurrent also the effective power to bring them into existence, immediately bringing the conceived elements into operative reality; there is no intervening time between the knowledge and its realization; but simultaneously and without time-interval, together with the willing is displayed also the work which is willed. In this way the will is effective power, so that whenever the existence of the existents is conceived (by God) the opportunity for the existence of the conceived existents is co-provided. So with reference to the creation, all of these are to be understood altogether instantaneously in God, i.e. the will, the wisdom, the effective power, and the actual existence of existents.[19]

Once Christians subscribe to the notion of God's *energeia* as the ground of all existence, they cannot use such concepts as "secularization", "desacralization", and "de-divinization" to mean the liberation of all things from any reference of God, the sacred or the divine. Rather than being liberated, all things, institutions, and persons would be reduced to nothing, for apart from the sacred and divine will of God nothing exists. Created existence is existence by participation in God's will: it is not autonomous or self-sufficient. Across the *diastema*, both humanity and nature participate in God's will. This is also Gregory's explanation for the constitution of matter: it is God's will, his energy, made palpable to our senses. God conceives and wills matter, and therein lies its mystery. We need to recover this concept in our time in order to find a new respect for inanimate as well as organic nature, viewing it as a dynamic movement of God's will and energy. The existence of all that is created is contingent upon the will of God. While his *ousia* remains transcendent, his *energeia* is the whole principle of existence — the immanent existence-giving, constitutive, teleological principle of the universe.

4. THE UNITY OF ALL CREATION

Though humanity shares in the fundamental nature of all creation, it does, according to Gregory, represent a unique element in God's creative process, with a unique constitution and a unique vocation.

Living in the 4th century, Gregory already had an elementary notion of biological evolution well ahead of his time.[20] Of course, he could not put forward a scientifically-based theory of the unity of all life and of progression in the character of the species. Nevertheless, he is able to say that organic life is a single whole, that the impulse of life ascended gradually from plants to animals to humanity, and that human nature incorporates the vegetative, the animal, and the rational. All elements in the created universe are both directly dependent on God for their very existence, and also totally interlinked with each other. What had been a standing doctrine among the Stoics with their understanding of the "conspiration" (*sympnoia*, breathing together) of the universe, and its *sympatheia* or experiencing everything as a whole, was now assimilated by Gregory into a Christian cosmology.[21] Because of his great respect for and unusual knowledge of medical science, he probably used Galen as his source, since this Greek-Roman medical scholar in a sense incorporated both Aristotle's notion of nature's gradual progress from inanimate to rational, and Poseidonius's doctrine of "seminal powers" in which the cosmos was conceived of as a living being able to create progressively more evolved creatures.

Gregory suggests that the creative energy of God appears to have taken a gradually ascending path, with humanity emerging at the last stage: "nature making the ascent, as though by steps. . . from the smallest to the things more perfect".[22] But although humankind appeared at the top of the ladder, it is not totally unrelated to or independent of the rest of the created world. While Gregory rejects the pagan attempt to understand man as a *mikrokosmos* which incorporates all the elements of the universe and thus becomes himself a little universe, he considers it important to see humanity in an integral relation to the universe of things, plants, and animals. While man does not derive the whole of his nature from the universe, he is an integral — and the most important — part of it, since he consciously links the universe to its creator.

This understanding of humanity as a mediator (*methorios*) between the animal and the divine has its root in the Platonic tradition, and was much used by Philo and Origen, to both of whom Gregory owes a great deal. But in neither Plato nor Poseidonius, nor even in Philo or Origen, is this concept raised to the noble Christian conception that humanity, in a conscious self-offering, lifts the whole created universe up to God. The emergence of Adam as body-soul was thus a terminal event in the evolution of the universe, a kind of full flowering and fruit bearing of the plant of the cosmos. The universe reveals its full nature only when it brings forth man; and after it has done so, God does not discard it, for it is on the plant of the universe that the human fruit subsists.[23]

It is the way humanity has dealt with the mediating position in which it has been placed that makes life so ambiguous and problematic.[24] Precisely because man is the image of God, freedom is the very essence of his being. He was offered every occasion to participate in and create the good. But he was under no compulsion to do so. Only by his voluntary choice of goodness could he become sovereign (*autokrates*) and free (*adespaton*).[25]

As a mediator between God and his creation, man has also been placed between good and evil. This is an inescapable part of being able to mediate in true freedom. Seeking to explain this human role, Gregory cites a tradition which refers to the universe as a double reality, part intelligible, part sensible, with conflicting qualities and characteristics.[26] Its intelligible nature (*noete physis*) is incorporeal, impalpable, formless; its sensible nature is the contrary. Although it is made up of opposites like fire and water, the universe remains a harmonious whole, because of the wisdom of God in which all opposing elements find reconciliation. In the same fashion, human nature is a harmonious combination of the sensible and the intelligible. God made the sensible part of man in order that the sensible part of the universe — which is also his creation — might, through its participation in man, participate freely in the good. But before man was created, the earth was in charge of an "angel" who was also created by God and endowed with glorious beauty and the freedom to exercise power. The angel's jealousy was aroused by the creation of man, who reflected the fullness of God's glory, out of the terrain that was subject to him. His jealousy, expressing a fall from the good, is the primary source of evil. He was created good, and when, by his free volition, he turned to evil, the lack or opposite of the good was created.

The placing of man between good and evil should not, Gregory insists, be interpreted as a parallel to his being placed between the intelligible and the sensible. He argues that the sensible is not the source of evil, but that the sentient part of man was the more susceptible to it. The poison of evil was mixed with the honey of sensual pleasure — the eating of the beautiful fruit of the tree of knowledge of good and evil — and thus entered our being. It has coarsened our bodies and made them heavy with the gravitational pull of sensuality, more akin to those of animals than were the light, airy, eukinetic (easy to move) bodies we originally had, which will be restored to us at the resurrection.[27] It is from this admixture of evil with our bodies and souls, and not from material or corporate existence, that we have to be saved and redeemed through the reconstitutive process of death and resurrection.

Since through his body and soul man becomes a participant in both the intelligible and the sensible, he is the citizen of two worlds, yet a whole being, with a special vocation to spread the grace of God through the whole of creation, animate and inanimate. He is superior to the angels, because, as he is made in the image of God, he can be open to the entire universe, the sensible as well as the intelligible.[28] He is akin to both God and matter, a member of both families, made to enjoy both the divine and the terrestrial. In him and through him, matter too is to be redeemed. That is why Christ became man and assumed a material body. Man in Christ is the Savior of the world: he restores it to God so that it may truly be filled with his glory.

5. THE FULLNESS OF HUMANITY

Gregory's basic conception of the unity of all humanity rings strangely in an age which tends to emphasize the primacy of the individual, so necessary to the capitalist, industrial system based on personal freedom, personal rights, and personal responsibility. His notion of the *pleroma* or the fullness of humanity therefore puts before us a challenge which we can ill afford to ignore.

The term *pleroma* itself comes from St. Paul, with Gnostic or Hellenistic antecedents. He speaks of the fullness of time, the fullness of God, the fullness of Christ. Jesus, the incarnate Christ, is the fullness of God. The very presence (*shekinah*) of God was pleased to dwell in a particular human being (Col. 1:19). True existence, full being, is present only in Christ out of the whole creation. In that sense, he supplies what is lacking in the creation: he gives it abiding and not merely transient being.

But Christ is *pleroma* in yet another sense. He is the link between God and his creation, for in him and by him and for him all things were created. The Gnostics spoke of *pleroma* as that which fills the gap. St. Paul, when he says that Christ is the *pleroma* of God, adds that the Church is the *pleroma* of Christ (Eph. 1:22-23). Here the *ecclesia* stands for the new humanity which, so to speak, "fills up" what is lacking in Christ. Christ, together with the new humanity—the "total Christ"—is the true *pleroma* that fills the gap between God's being and the universe, and participates fully in both.

This is the great mystery of humanity—Christ in us, we in Christ. As we are identified as members of his body, Christ stands as the mediator between God and the universe. This is the true rationale for Gregory's understanding of the platonic notion of man as *methorios* or mediator between God and the universe, as taking the creation into God and God into the creation, breaking across all *diastema*. And when Christ is formed in us, when we are fully grounded and rooted in love, then we are filled with the whole fullness of God himself.

Gregory takes this late Pauline understanding of *pleroma* and applies it in a double sense to humanity as a whole. For him, what is called humanity is not individual men and women, but the whole of it in all space and all time, all races and all nations, past, present, and future:

> Just as a single human being is circumscribed by the size of his body, and his individual existence is denoted by the measure of his body, so also it seems to me the whole (*pleroma*) of humanity is held as a single body, by the foreknowing creative power of God over all existents. And this is what the word teaches when it says, 'And God made man, and according to the image of God He made him.' For

the image is not in a part of the (human) nature, nor is the grace in any one of the conceptions subsumed under it. Rather, this creative power of God extends equally to the whole human race. The sign of this is the fact that all are endowed with mind. All alike have the power to understand and to will and to do all those other things through which the divine nature is reflected in that which is made in its image. There can be no essential difference between man as was manifested at the beginning of the formation of the world and as will be manifested towards the consummation of the world-process; they would equally bear the image of God. Because of this, the whole is named one man, for in the creative power of God there is nothing that is past or future, for his power is effective equally over what to us is the past or the future. Thus, then, the whole nature from the first to the last together constitute one single image of Him Who Is.[29]

For Gregory, the fullness of time is coterminous with the fullness of humanity. Both must together come to an end. When the whole *pleroma* of humanity as originally conceived by the creator is fully unfoldled, time and history will come to a close:

When the formation of man is completed, time also should terminate; then comes the total reconstitution of the whole universe; along with the transformation of the whole shall take place the reconstitution of human existence, from the earth-bound and corruptible to the impassible and eternal.[30]

History, then, is the springtime of the Spirit. It is the time for ploughing by repentance and for sowing seed by heeding the word of God. History is certainly not the final reality, but neither is it a meaningless illusion. It is to be taken as seriously as the field to be ploughed in which the seed is to be scattered. But ultimately it is not the field and the plant that matter, but the grain or fruit which is borne on the plant and which will be gathered together in the final harvest. The new metahistorical existence, the new creation, into which the whole of humanity has to be reborn through death and resurrection, has already been inaugurated through Christ's death, resurrection, and ascension. He has assumed all humankind into himself, and exalted it to the right hand of God.

This unity of Christ with all humanity is the great mystery of the Gospel. Christ, the Emmanuel, is the new creation, the new humanity. All that is good in humanity, old or new, is assimilated into the new man; the good in the whole human *pleroma* is of Christ.

It is important to note that, for Gregory, there is no contradiction between *via crucis* and *via gloriae*. The cross is our glory; there is no way to the glory of the resurrection except through suffering and death. But the most significant distinction between Gregory's conception and that of Augustine is that, for the former, the glory of man is not a rival for the glory of God, but rather is identical with it. It is in Christ's humanity that God is glorified. So when man truly manifests the wisdom, the power, and the love of God, his glory shows forth the glory of God.

Since the incarnation of Jesus Christ, God and man are not "totally other". Across the gap between the creation and the creator, the creator God has come in person. The whole status of creation was transformed when the creator crossed the *diastema*, and through the tearing of his own body opened the way for us who were on the other side of the veil to enter the holy of holies and be present with Christ at the right hand of God (Eph. 12:6). Not as individuals, however, but as the whole *pleroma* are we to experience this moving across the *diastema* into the presence of God.

6. THE HUMAN VOCATION IN TIME AND SPACE

At the 1959 Patristic Conference at Oxford, the French Benedictine father, R. Gillet, read a paper entitled, "Man as Cosmic Divinizer in the Thought of St. Gregory of Nyssa".[31] The term "divinizer", which does not come from Gregory's writings but is Gillet's own creation, seems to be in particular contrast with current trends which see the role of humanity as "de-divinizing" the cosmos and secularizing institutions and ideas.

Gregory himself does not even use the term *theosis* or divinization to designate what *happens* to humanity; he rather holds that man becomes divine in the measure in which he becomes conformed to God through developing the "qualities" of God, that is, the good. But what does "the good" mean? Here he uses three central terms: *eleutheria* (freedom), *apatheia* (nonpassivity), and *areté* (effective practice of the good). Freedom, inseparable from the other two qualities—*apatheia* and *areté*—is the very essence of God, and the major constituent of the "image of God" in which man is made:

Freedom is the *ecsimilation* (*exhomoiosis*)[32] to that which is self-determining (*adespoton*)[33] and sovereign (*autokrates*), which was the nature endowed upon us by God in the beginning, but now, along with the shame of our sin, obscured. All freedom is in one sense one by nature, connatural with itself. It follows, therefore, that all that is free will be coharmonized with all else that is similarly free. Virtue (*arete*) is self-determining. And all that is free is in this same virtue, for freedom is self-determining.[34]

Virtue, then, means practice of the good, and only that which is good by self-determination is truly good. This is why it is impossible for Gregory to accept the notion of a sovereign grace which comes from outside and compels man to do good. Here he is definitely anti-Augustinian: for him man is not simply a most obedient servant of God. Nor can he conceive of the doing of good works as a *means* to salvation, for then salvation would become something other than the good, and the good merely an instrument to achieve it. Gregory clarifies his concept of goodness in *On the Making of Man*:

> God is by nature everything whatever we are able to conceive of the good. Rather, he surpasses and transcends everything we can conceive or apprehend of the good; and even for the creation of human life, there is no other reason but that He is good. This being thus, and since this is why he was impelled to fashion human nature, it was not in some half measure that He manifested the creative power of his goodness, endowing part of his own goodness while holding back participation in the other part out of jealousy. But the idea of the fullness of his goodness means that, in leading man out of non-being into being, God made him complete and not lacking anything (*anendee*) for working out the good.
>
> The list of all these (divine) good qualities would be too long, and number cannot exhaust such a list. Therefore the word, resuming all the good under one comprehensive term, says that man was made in the image of God. This is equivalent to saying that He made human nature participant in all good.
>
> If the divine is the fullness (*pleroma*) of all good, this (human nature) is the icon or image of that. And the resemblance of the icon to the original, therefore, consists in being the fullness of all good. Thus in us is the idea or seminal possibility of all good, all virtue and wisdom, and everything whatever that one can conceive of as exalted and noble.
>
> One of these many qualities must of necessity be to be free and not to be subjugated to any natural power, but to be self-authoritative (*autexousion*), to direct the will to what is freely chosen. For virtue is something which is self-ruled (*adespoton*) and voluntary. That which is compelled or forced can never be virtue.[35]

This human freedom, of which *apatheia* and *aretē* are only two aspects, is not completely identical with the freedom of God. There is a difference between the archetype and the icon. It consists primarily in the fact that God is what He wills to be, and does not will something other than He is. So God's nature is in no need of change, while the only thing which is constant about the image, that is, man, is that it is in a continuous process of change. Gregory insists that such change belongs to all created existence, and that man must continue to change even beyond death. For the good in which he is to grow has no bounds or limits which can be reached at a particular time. There is infinite possibility within the good, and man must continue, in freedom, to grow infinitely.

Gregory qualifies this notion of permanent and infinite change by pointing out that continuous change does not mean the absence of any continuity except that of change. Our created identity remains. Just as our personal identity remains the same throughout the continuing change in our physical body, so it also endures through death and resurrection, and the imprint of what we have done in the body remains indelibly on our souls.[36] The physical body and what we do with it determines the character of the soul. History determines the character of meta-history.

7. DOMINION OVER THE CREATION

Gregory insists on God's intention that man, as his sensible or visible icon, participating in his qualities *nous* (mind) and *phronesis* (discernment or wisdom), should have as the basis for his existence a body, thus enabling matter itself to participate in the structure of God's self-manifestation.[37] Mind does not exist without a body, just as music cannot be produced without an instrument. God allows the material to participate in the spiritual by making the former the basis for the latter; and just as the soul in man cannot be located in any part of the body, but pervades the whole of it, so man, as the image of God, is to pervade the whole universe, to regulate it, to "hominize" it, as Teilhard put it.

Interpreting the command of Genesis 1:6, that man should have "dominion over the fish of the sea, and over the fowl of the air, and over the cattle, and over all the earth, and over every creeping thing that creepeth on the earth", Gregory emphasizes that humanity must acquire such dominion, or kingship, as he calls it, by its own effort. We best see the royal stature of man in those who have become really free by learning to control their own wills. When man wears the purple of virtue and the crown of justice, he becomes a living image of the King of kings, of God himself.[38] The beauty of God is the beauty of joy, of beatitude, of blessedness. God is love, and where love is absent in man, his image disappears. God is Word and Spirit; so man is endowed with mind and reason. His ability to perceive and express, to will and to act, to envision and imagine, to love and to create makes man truly human. But the mind can develop fully only as the body grows. Yet, since our heads are erect, our hands freed from the need to support the body, and our tongues released from the task of taking food from the ground, we can use our heads to think, our tongues to speak, and our hands in the service of our heads.[39]

Thus the mind's proper functioning is dependent on man becoming free, just, righteous, fully engaged in creating the good. If all human activities and abilities, including the development of science and technology, were subordinated to and integrated with the quest for justice, freedom, peace, and creative goodness, the human rule over the creation could mean a blessing for the whole universe.

CHAPTER SIX

The Eastern Tradition Continues

1. THE DIONYSIAN WRITINGS

Though, after Gregory of Nyssa, there are in the Eastern tradition few highly influential formulations of the general framework of reality, some of the most outstanding among them should be briefly introduced here.

An important monument in the Eastern tradition is the thought of that mysterious figure who called himself Dionysius the Areopagite after the 1st-century convert and disciple of St. Paul. Dionysius, though fully Christian, was less critical in his adoption of Platonism, taking his cues largely from Proclus, the encyclopaedic and perhaps the last great pagan thinker in the Neoplatonist school. Dionysius was translated into Latin in the 9th century by Scotus Erigena, and, with the borrowed authority of the 1st-century disciple of St. Paul, became uniquely authoritative in the West for what was later to develop as "mystical theology". He was certainly also influential in the East, but not to the same extent.

The concept of "mediation" plays a central role in his thought. It is not as individuals that human beings are transformed. Rather, as they participate in the ordered community around God, receiving and transmitting in the measure of their own capacity his creative energy and life-giving light, they are made more and more conformed

73

to his image. Both the corporate element and the double aspect of receiving and transmitting were largely overlooked in the West. The neologism, *hierarcheia*, which he seems to have been the first to use extensively, was also misunderstood in the West. He did not mean hierarchy as a scale of authority, or a pyramidal structure of command and obedience. His central insight was that of *ordering* in the sense of structuring rather than of commanding. The divine society around God, in which the deifying powers were operative, was an orderly, dynamic, light-receiving-and-transmitting society, in which the whole cosmos, including unbelievers, participated. Dionysius's hierarchy did not exclude the laity or even the unbaptized.

But Dionysius cannot be considered a pillar of the Eastern tradition, primarily because in his hierarchy he places humanity lower than the angels. Yet he has exerted a decisive influence in the Byzantine tradition, especially on the thought of Maximus the Confessor, Andrew of Crete, George Pachymeres, and Gregory Palamas. His influence can be seen also in the thought of mystics of the West like Thomas à Kempis, Eckhart, and Tauler, as well as in the great thinkers of the Middle Ages like Albertus Magnus and Thomas Aquinas.

2. THE TOWERING FIGURE
OF THE BYZANTINE TRADITION:
MAXIMUS THE CONFESSSOR

Within the Byzantine tradition, the decisively towering figure is that of Maximus the Confessor, who resigned the post of imperial secretary under Emperor Heraclius to become a monk. Though not acknowledged by the universal tradition (for, by his time, the Church was already divided between the Graeco-Latins and the Asian-Africans), his cosmological thought embodies some of the best insights of the Eastern tradition.

One of the most stimulating studies on Maximus is by Hans Urs von Balthasar in his *Liturgie Cosmique*.[1] His anthropology has been studied comprehensively by Lars Thunberg in his *Microcosm and Mediator*.[2] Balthasar obviously regarded Origen, Gregory of Nyssa, and Maximus as the pillars on which the patristic tradition was erected. In his preface to the book on Maximus, he asks whether or not the questions posed today by existentialism and idealism were not more fruitfully raised and discussed by Gregory and Maximus, of course in the context of their own world, but in a manner that illuminates also our own existence today.

Maximus represents the full flowering of Greek Christian thought, compared to which even a much later Byzantine thinker like Gregory Palamas seems to be a step backwards. Maximus follows the lines set by Gregory and Dionysius: the whole world is penetrated by the *energeia* of God, while God himself remains beyond the luminous cloud, unknown by name, incomprehensible to our minds, transcending not only the understanding, but also beyond all being and all good.

Maximus's greatest contribution lies in developing further the idea that one finds in both Gregory and Dionysius: that man is a mediator between God and the cosmos. The idea of mediation and intermediary beings belongs to the Greek tradition as a whole. We see it in sharper relief in the Plotinian school of paganism and in Origen's school among the Christians. In middle Platonism the intermediary beings constituted an ascending scale of participation with each level participating in the level immediately above it, while the final level, the *nous* or world-soul participated in God himself, or in the One. It was by this scheme that the smallest grain of sand could be linked up to the power of God which holds it in existence.

Gregory of Nyssa had introduced into this continuity of the All with the One an element of discontinuity—the great abyss of *diastema* between the creator and the creation. In the thought of Maximus, too, this tension between the immanence of God in the world by his *energeia* and the transcendence of God in the freedom of his *ousia* plays a central role.

By his Spirit, God is in his entirety present in both the *katholon* (the whole) and the *idion* (the particular), but without limiting his being to either the one or the other. This concept, while providing us with a unified structure of God and cosmos, still maintains the dualism between God and the cosmos, between that in which everything participates—God, and that which participates—the cosmos and its diverse constituents including humanity. Not the reciprocity of subject and object, but that of creative love and response, is the fundamental rhythm of reality. This reciprocity is not confined to the cosmos alone. Passivity is not dead objectivity, but an active response. Matter is not resistant, as in pagan Greek thought, but responsive. Maximus contradicts Aristotle's conception of pure act as reality. Reality is active-passive, creative-responsive. Passivity and receptivity are not imperfections, but expressions of the created capacity to respond to the creator.

God, as immanent, is the true being of all beings. God, as transcendent, is beyond being, nonbeing as source of all being. His *energeia* is manifest in creation. His *ousia* is beyond all manifest being. Affirmations about God relate to his *energeia*; about his *ousia* only negation is possible. But the affirmation and the negation have to be held together. This is where the Christian tradition expresses a subtle difference from the negative theologies of Hinduism and Buddhism. "*Neti, neti*" (not this, not this), the Eastern Christian tradition and the Hindu-Buddhist tradition agree in saying about God. But the Christian tradition insists that the negation is not the whole truth, that it becomes truth only when held in tension with the affirmation of the world as created and sustained by the *energeia* of God. Both being and nonbeing are dimensions of God in his immanence-transcendence.

Since our main interest is in seeing the relation between man and cosmos, we shall limit our brief study of Maximus to a few of his central cosmological-anthropological conceptions. It is important for us to see how Maximus takes the Eastern tradition back to the Platonic world of ideas, from which Gregory of Nyssa had sought to rescue Christian thought. Nyssa, in denying a "world of ideas" different from the world of particulars, had made the epistemological problem quite acute. Both Balthasar and von Ivanka are of the view that Gregory of Nyssa cannot give us a comprehensible view of how it is possible for man to intuit essences except in terms of universal ideas.[3] Maximus puts the ideas back into the primordial creative conception of God, which is then, as in Origen, identified with the Logos as the second person of the Trinity:

> In God the ideas (*logoi*) of all things are fixed; thus it is said that God knows all things before they come forth, for they are in him and with him as he is the very truth of all that exists; even things in their totality, i.e. those that are and those that are yet to be, do not come into existence simultaneously with their ideas which God has in his knowledge, but each one comes into existence at the time pre-determined for it...All things created are defined, both in their being and in their becoming, by their own particular ideas or *logoi* and by the ideas of other existents which are externally proximate to them, and the existents are thus circumscribed by their ideas.[4]

But this multiplicity of *logoi* is constituted by a single *logos* which is their unifying principle. The *logos* in its unity is transcendent, while in its multiplicity it remains immanent in particular existents. This has important consequences for Maximus's anthropology. For humanity, too, in this conception, becomes predetermined by the idea of man, and to that extent the concept of freedom plays a lesser role in Maximus than in Gregory. The purpose of Maximus is of course to define humanity by its original model, namely the divine Logos himself who became the Son of Man. The imitation of Christ thus becomes the central ethical norm for Maximus. The measure of our conformity to Jesus Christ is the measure in which we are human.

In continuity with insights of the patristic tradition, Maximus insists, however, that God knows things not because of their ideas but because they are products of his will. The ideas coexist in the mind of God, and are brought into existence as particulars by his will. So the ideas themselves are now the products of God's will, or, to put it more precisely, the idea and the existence of each particular have their root in the will of God.

Consequently, Maximus conceives the relationship of the particular to the totality (the *idion* to the *katholon*) also in the will of God. Thus, particular events in history are not mere shadows of the world of ideas; each substance and event in the whole has also a relationship to the whole which is willed by God. The relationship (*schesis*) of each to others is rooted in the difference from others which constitutes its particularity. God is the guardian of both the relationship and the difference. Nonidentity with others is what guarantees the identity of each. Dissimilarity protects the entity of particulars and constitutes an essential character of the world. But dissimilarity and the identity based on it can be properly held only in relationship to other particulars and to the whole. Identity does not imply independence.

This is a distinctive character of created existence, according to Maximus, not simply "to be", but "to be in a particular way". Simply to be is possible only for God. A created being 'is' only in a particularly qualified way, in a particular relationship to others. Each occupies a particular place and time and is distinguished by its particular qualities.

Maximus comes very close to some of our modern insights about the nature of space and time. He thinks the idea of infinite space or infinite time is self-contradictory. But space and time are not so much physico-astronomical realities as ontological limitations of existence. Both extension and duration are indications of finitude for Maximus. Here he is unlike Gregory of Nyssa, who could think of an infinite duration in which there can be infinite progress in the good for created beings. According to Maximus, temporality and finitude go together, and when man experiences full salvation, he will move out of temporality into eternity, which is the proper mode or existence of God himself.

Unlike Gregory of Nyssa, who regards change (*tropē*) and movement (*kinesis*) as essential aspects of created existence, Maximus sees a human being progressing by movement (*kinesis*) from birth (*genesis*) to fullness of being (*stasis*), that is, existence which is enjoyed without duration and extension. In the *aion* to come (John of Scythopolis had interpreted *aion* as derived from *aei on* eternally existing) there is perfect rest.

Balthasar shows us how for Maximus the trilogy *genesis-kinesis-stasis* is paralleled by the other trilogy to-be, to-be-good, to-be-forever, *einai, eu einai, aei einai*.[5] For Maximus, becoming is only the beginning. Once you have become what you are, there is not further need of beginning. Once you have become what you are, there is not further need of becoming. In this trilogy, "to-be" and "to-be-forever" are the gift of God, while "to-be-good" needs the contribution of our own free wills. Our created existence, as becoming, is the movement from *genesis* to *stasis* through the free cooperation of the will in the ascent towards the good. Eternal life is the boundary of becoming. Like Augustine, Maximus writes in an era of world-weariness, when rest appears to be the highest good, and static salvation becomes the ideal.

Among the important elements in Maximus's thought is also his vision of the "salvation of things". He argues:

> It is necessary that this world of things dies, just as a man dies, in order that it may rise again, young instead of old as it was before death . . . And we who are man will also rise up, as part of the whole, as a small world within the big universe. [Humanity and the universe] shall receive the definitive quality of incorruptibility, the body receiving a new form identical with that of the soul, and sensible things will have a form identical with spiritual things, as the divine power, which is beyond all things, in a manifest and efficacious presence will spread its force on each thing according to its capacity and hold all things together in its divine embrace, in an inseparable union, for all eternity.[6]

Only when humanity comes into the fullness of its own salvation is matter also set free from its bondage to death, as St. Paul said to the Romans. Christ will assume all things in himself, uniting the whole creation in himself, through the mediation of man.

This idea of man as mediator between God and cosmos has been ably interpreted by Lars Thunberg.[7] He speaks of a five-fold mediation:

a)   *Between man and woman*: Christ was both male and female in one. Man must mediate not by eliminating the feminine qualities and replacing them by masculine ones or *vice-versa*. He must become fully human in a male-female way by the combination and sublimation of all male and female characteristics of human nature.

b)   *Between paradise and oikoumene*: Paradise is the community of the good, of justice and peace, of virtue and righteousness. Man in Christ is to mediate between this and the inhabited earth (*oikoumene*) by manifesting and embodying the life of paradise upon this earth. Man is to practice a "God-like way of life" and thereby mediate between paradise and history. This way of life is manifested primarily in relation to others and in self-discipline, through voluntary suffering, and through labor.

c)   *Between heaven and earth*: The gap between the realm of heaven where God's will is obeyed, and this earth where it is not, is to be bridged in man. The ascension of Christ into the heavens is the great symbol of this human entrance into the realm beyond the boundary of our immediate sense-perception. Man must, while living on earth, be able to ascend to heaven, and thus become the ladder that connects heaven and earth. When man breaks away from dependence on his earthly impulses, he is able to know the *logoi* or ideas of sensible realities, and from thence to ascend by contemplation to the unity of the *Logos* who is behind the *logoi*.

d)   *Between the intelligible and the sensible*: Closely linked to the third mediating function, but distinct from it, is man's vocation to be the mediator between matter and spirit. Christ takes his body with him into the heavenly realm. In man, matter enters the realm of the spirit. Humanity is led to the boundary of its knowledge of sensible realities, and is under pressure to go beyond the confines of space and time, to the *Logos* itself which underlies and activates that space-time world of sensible realities. It is in the eucharist that man enters the presence of God: closing the doors of history and science, but remaining in his body, he communes in the body and blood of the ascended Lord.

e)   *Between God and his creation*: Here Christ is again the central principle. It is through love that this mediation is effected. When man gives himself to God's love and is united with him by grace, man penetrates entirely into God, and becomes God, without losing his identity as man. In Christ, God has become man and man has become God. Through ecstatic love, this union of God and man in Christ is realized again and again in human experience. Here concepts and thoughts have to give place to "mystical union". Man and God enter into an act of love and union which implies *communicatio idiomatum*, the participation in the qualities and mode of existence of the one by the other, and a mutual *perichoresis*,[8] that is, a mutual interpenetration which unites God and man without destroying their identity. This penetration takes place on behalf of the whole creation, yet it transcends the creation, effecting a unity across the *diastema* that divides the creator from the creation. It is achieved only by grace, though such grace is prepared for by self-purification and the act of the human will yearning and striving after God. The chasm between the creator and his creation is not abolished, but it is bridged by an act of mutual love sustained by God's grace and the responding free will of humanity. Both, in effect, go out of themselves to reach out to the other and find union in love.

3. RECENT EASTERN CHRISTIAN REFLECTION ON THE HUMAN ROLE IN GOD'S CREATION

Since Maximus the Confessor, only a little progress has been made in the Eastern tradition. There is the scholastic systematization of patristic thought in John of Damascus, its ascetical working out in Gregory of Palamas, its liturgical interpretation in Nicolas Cabasilas, but none of this attains the grandeur of conception characteristic of Gregory, Dionysius, and Maximus.

When we come nearer to our own times, we find the extraordinary figure of 19th-century Russian spirituality, the lyrical prophet of humanity, Vladimir Solovyev.[9] The central notion of his works is the vision of humanity as one. The image of *sophia* or wisdom stands at once for the whole of creation in space and time, for the whole of humanity in space and time, and for the whole of the Church in space and time. Solovyev was an ecumenist well before his time, one whose vision of the eventual unity and mutual complementarity of the three main traditions of Christianity—the Eastern Orthodox, the Roman Catholic, and the Protestant Reformed—still inspires. He was as much involved in the political and economic thought of his time as he was in philosophy, theology, art, and literature. Solovyev was a fighter for justice and peace, consciously opposing the Tolstoyan attitude of nonresistance to evil. He considered the struggle between good and evil an essential part of history, and the typical Eastern Orthodox theology which sought to steer clear of this life-and-death struggle in society seemed irrelevant to his sensitive mind.

Solovyev saw clearly the two opposing tendencies in Western life, one seeking to glorify man at the expense of God, the other seeking to glorify God by denigrating the human—the conflict between Renaissance optimism and Augustinian pessimism. Between these two spirits, the West never really achieved a creative synthesis, though there were scattered efforts like those of Erasmus, Nicolas of Cusa, and St. Francis de sales. It is in this context that Solovyev advances as a universal principle the idea of God-manhood, which has its roots in the Old Testament conception, of *hochmah*, *sophia*, wisdom. Wisdom or *sophia* existed before the creation of the world, eternally in the bosom of the Father, along with the *logos*. The *logos* is the producing principle; *sophia* is the actualizing one.

Applying the principle that the whole is prior to its parts and is presupposed by them, Solovyev insists that the whole of humanity is prior to individual human beings, and thus constitutes one organic whole. He then concludes that *sophia* "is no other than the true, pure, and perfect humanity, the highest and all-embracing form and the living soul of nature and the universe, united to God from all eternity and in the temporal process attaining union with him and uniting to him all that is".[10]

In the redemption of man, therefore, the redemption of nature is directly implied, says Solovyev, long before our ecological crisis broke out:

> What is needed in the first instance is that we should treat our social and cosmic environment as an actual living being with which we are in the closest and most complete inter-action, without ever being merged in it. . . In order that [the false separation of beings in space and time] should be abolished altogether, and all individuals, both past and present, should finally become eternal, the process of integration must transcend the limits of social or strictly human life and include the cosmic sphere from which it started.

In ordering the physical world the divine idea threw the veil of natural beauty over the kingdom of matter and death; through man, through the activity of his universally rational consciousness, it must enter that kingdom *from within* in order to give life to nature and make its beauty eternal. In this sense it is essential to change man's relation to nature. He must enter with it too into the same relation of syzygic unity which determines his true life in the personal and social sphere.

Nature has so far been either an omnipotent despotic mother of the child man, or a slave, a thing foreign to him. In that second epoch (of western thought) poets alone preserved and kept up a timid and unconscious love for nature as a being possessing full rights and having, or capable of having, life in itself...

To establish a truly loving or syzygic relation between man and his natural and cosmic, as well as his social environment is a purpose that is quite clear in itself. But the same thing cannot be said about the ways in which an individual man can attain it. Without going into premature and therefore dubious and unsuitable details, one can confidently say one thing on the basis of well-established analogies from cosmic and historical experience. Every conscious human activity, determined by the idea of universal syzygy and having for its purpose the embodiment of the all-embracing ideal in some particular here, actually produces or liberates spiritually-material currents which gradually gain possession of the material environment, spiritualize it and embody in it certain images of the all-embracing unity.[11]

Solovyev holds the view that love is the relationship that should characterize not only interpersonal relations, but also our relation to the cosmic environment. Our love creates spiritual energies which inwardly transform the cosmos itself, imprinting upon it the image of God as love. The cosmos itself is a living organism within which the *pleroma* of humanity as an organ has a central and key function almost like the heart or the brain in the body. *Sophia* is both humanity and the earth-principle, the *magna mater*. The constitution of humanity itself is as a mediating principle between God and nature.

The Orthodox churches of the 20th century have been reluctant to accept the teaching of Solovyev as being within the authentic tradition. There are many elements in his speculative sophilogy, no doubt, which are alien to the tradition. But, essentially, Solovyev belongs to the tradition of Gregory of Nyssa, Dionysius, and Maximus. Especially in his insistence on man as mediator between God and creation, and on the redemption of creation being bound up with the redemption of man, Solovyev remains faithful to the authentic tradition which begins in this regard with the Apostle Paul in Romans and Colossians.

When we go beyond Solovyev to our own century, it is striking how little attention is given by Orthodox theologians to issues relating to the human role within the cosmos. Only a few articles have been devoted to topics such as creation, nature, and time.[12] All the writers, however, point to the fact that human redemption is inseparable from the redemption of time and space as well as of "things". One quotation from Olivier Clément's article on "L'homme dans le monde" may exemplify and illustrate this general emphasis in today's authentic voice of the Eastern tradition:

> If the spiritual destiny of man is inseparable from that of humanity (as a whole), it is also inseparable from that of the terrestrial cosmos. The sensible universe as a whole constitutes, in fact, a prolongation of our bodies. Or rather, what is our body, if it is not the form imprinted by our 'living soul' on the universal 'dust' which increasingly penetrates and traverses us? There is no discontinuity between the flesh of the world and human flesh; the universe participates in human nature, as it constitutes the body of humanity. . . Man is the hypostasis [personality] of the cosmos, its conscious and personal self-expression; it is he who gives meaning to things and who has to transfigure them. For the universe, man is its hope to receive grace and to be united with God; Man is also the possibility of failure and loss for the universe. Let us recall the fundamental text of St Paul in Romans 8:22. Subject to disorder and death by our fall, the creation waits also for man's becoming Son of God by grace, which would mean liberation and glory for it also. We are responsible for the world, to the very smallest twigs and plants. We are the word, the 'logos' by which the world expresses itself, by which the world speaks to God: it depends on us whether it blasphemes or it prays, whether it becomes an illusion or wisdom, black magic or celebration. Only through us, can the cosmos, as the prolongation of our bodies, have access to eternity. How strange all this must sound to modern minds! That is our evil, our sin, our freedom led astray to vampirize nature; it is we who are responsible for the carcasses and the twisted trees that pollution produces, it is our refusal to love that baffles the sad eyes of so many animals. But every time a human being becomes aware of the cosmic significance of the eucharist, each time a pure being receives a humble sensation with gratitude — whether he eats a fruit or inhales the fragrance of the earth — a sort of joy of eternity reverberates in the marrow of things.[13]

CHAPTER SEVEN

Mastery and Mystery

In a symposium on "Man and Technology" organized some years ago at the University of Lausanne by the International Academy of the Philosophy of Science, the now familiar point was made that our technological civilization is creating and sustaining its own world view. As the introduction to the report of the symposium[1] states it:

> According to the conception of our ancestors, the highest form of knowledge, which ennobled man, was contemplative knowledge. It was on the basis of this knowledge that the highest form of religious life was conceived. The ultimate goal of man was conceived as being of a contemplative nature, and was termed the beatific vision. But in the new conception (of a technological civilization), the highest form of knowledge is that which gives man the greatest mastery over the forces of nature.
>
> In the old conception, two principal actors had entered the stage — God and man, God being preeminent over man. In today's Promethean conception, two actors are again on the stage — man and nature, man being predominant over nature. In both cases, man intervenes. But, in the first case, it is man as submissive to God. We can thus speak of an essentially religious *Weltanschauung* (worldview). In the second case, it is man as sovereign over technical works which have come out of his own creative hands. Here we are in the presence of a secularization of the old *Weltanschauung*. This is the basic cultural problem that confronts our contemporaries today.[2]

In the measure in which the foregoing analysis is true, the death of God is a fact in our civilization. Man has asserted his independence, overthrown God, and created his own universe with himself at the center. Whether it is God who is dead, or the civilization (and therefore man) which is dying, is open to debate.

But is the analysis true? Were there only two principal actors on the stage? The fact that the religious thinkers held contemplation to be the highest form of knowledge and the beatific vision the goal of all life, does not necessarily mean that the whole civilization was acting on that premise. Certainly, if the world is the stage, even in old times there were always more than two actors on the stage. Nature was there, feeding man, worked upon by man, developing his body and mind, developed by the body and mind of man. Culture and history were there on the stage, shaping and being shaped by man. The dialectic between man and nature had been there as long as man had existed, whether God was consciously acknowledged or not. In that sense, we have to revise the hypothesis of Professor Dockx, and say that there were three principal actors on the stage in the first scene — nature, world, and God.

The problem for man was that perhaps he did not like the presence of God, who seemed to stand in the way of his dominating nature, of his exploiting it for his own purposes. It was especially inconvenient since the theologians kept saying that man must make minimum use of nature and things, and concentrate on God. God became, in such a conception, a rival claimant for man's attention. The Christian Church, too, kept saying that man should not be materialistic, but should turn to God or to "spiritual values" as the possessions to be coveted most. The fact that the most powerful supporters and advocates of adherence to spiritual values were the already rich upper and middle classes, who made exhortations to love your neighbor, to practice patience, self-control, and nonviolence, to think and to learn, made them seem suspiciously hypocritical to the masses. They looked suspiciously like means for keeping the poor in want and dependence, while the spiritual elite continued to own most of the property and the liquid wealth. The problem of the rivalry between God and things was created by a theology which was mainly the product of the affluent and of the ascetics whom they supported and encouraged.

Today, we need to overcome this basic rivalry between God and things. But it is not the only one that needs to be overcome — the rivalry between man and God is just as much a problem. It seems to have been assumed that the glory of God was in inverse proportion to the glory of man. The more man abased himself, the more God was glorified. This theory was reinforced by the doctrine of original sin. All men were sinners and nothing but sinners, so all they could do was to confess their faults, practice humility, and make themselves of no account.

Let us think first about the rivalry between God and things. The assumption of three actors on a stage — nature, man, and God — is so presented that we get the impression that man must turn his back on God in order to address himself to a scientific-technological relation with so-called subhuman nature, and conversely, turn his back on subhuman nature, if he is to address himself humbly to the sovereign God.

This image is as faulty as it is misleading. In the first place, nature, man, and God are not three disjunct realities on the stage with a space-interval between their respective boundaries. Man is part of nature, and, at least as long as he is in space-time and remains a body-soul integral entity, he can never get outside nature and from that point choose what to do with it. Nature itself is in fact the stage, complete with the actors and props among which man is placed. He cannot turn away from it, as long as he has to occupy some space, whether in a city or in the desert, as long as he has to breathe, eat, drink, and eliminate his wastes. Man's life interpenetrates nature in the old or any other possible civilization.

Secondly, God is not a reality with precise physical boundaries; man cannot create a space-time interval between himself and God. God is the reality which sustains both man and nature, and it is through man himself and through nature that God presents himself to man. In this sense, it is foolish to see God and nature as alternative poles placed so that if man turns towards one he must turn his back on the other.

For this reason, I believe it is wrong to set man's domination of nature over against his stewardship of it. Replacing the concept of domination with the concept of stewardship will not lead us very far, for even in the latter there lies the hidden possibility of the objectification and alienation which are the root causes of the sickness of our civilization. Nature would remain some kind of property, owned not by us, of course, but by God, given into our hands for efficient and productive use. We would still be operating within the ambit of what Theodore Roszak calls single vision. We would still be reducing nature to "nothing but. . .", that is, nothing but an object given into our hands for safe keeping and good management. The parable of the talents cannot be interpreted to give New Testament support to the concept of the stewardship of nature, for there is no indication in the parable that the ten, five, and one talents given to the different servants signify nature. They could much more credibly signify the potentialities of each person. It would also be a theological mistake to use Genesis 1:21 as the basis for substituting the stewardship concept for the domination concept with which theology has operated in the past in relation to nature. The question goes much deeper than the good management of something outside ourselves.

The inclusive-exclusive argument has more point precisely because objectification-alienation is directly involved in the exclusivist position. There is no use blaming the Hebrews for this position. While it is true that the people of Israel had a stringent mandate from their God to turn from the worship of various nature gods and to pursue exclusively the cult of the transcendent Yahweh, it should not be concluded that such a jealous monotheism somehow ruled out all respect for nature as the creation of God. The mountains and trees shout for joy and tremble with fear at the approach of Yahweh, and the praises of God rise from nature and man alike to blend in a cosmic symphony. The Hebrews did not so separate themselves from all nature-symbolism as to concentrate solely on something we call "history" for which they had no word. They made no such distinctions as those between nature and history, nature and grace, nature and supernature. Nature simply served the purpose of God, as when the land gives increase to the seed, and the sea becomes dry land for Israel to pass over. It is we who have made these false distinctions which remain part and parcel of our disastrous theological equipment, which if applied effectively would be more harmful than the polluted air of our cities.

For those who understand the incarnation of Jesus Christ, the inclusive-exclusive debate should not be difficult to resolve. It was matter that Christ assumed to constitute his "historical" body; it was food that he ate, water or wine that he drank, air that he breathed, the earth and sea on which he walked. It was of the elements of the earth that his body was constituted, the body which was transfigured on Mount Tabor, crucified on the tree, and came out through the mouth of the tomb, the body in which he appeared to his disciples, in which he ascended to heaven. Matter and nature participate in the redemption, as St. Paul clearly tells us in Romans 8, no matter how hard modern exegetical gymnastics may try to prove that by the expression "all creation" he means only the whole of humankind.

The exclusive-inclusive debate is a false problem. God includes the whole universe in his creation as well as in redemption in Christ. This does not remove all distinctions between humanity and the rest of creation. Humanity has a special vocation as the priest of creation, as the mediator through whom God manifests himself to creation and redeems it. But this does not make humanity totally discontinuous with creation, since a priest has to be an integral part of the people he represents. Christ has become part of creation, and in his created body he lifted up the creation to God, and humankind must participate in this eternal priesthood of Christ.

TECHNOLOGY AND SACRAMENT

Heidegger defined theology as an ontic, not an ontological discipline, an attempt to interpret the phenomenon of Christianity as an objective phenomenon in the world. He obviously remembered some things about Christianity from his youthful seminary days. But it is hard to understand how he could have been so blind to the simple fact that what he tries to do in his philosophy is precisely what the Christian tries to do in his reflection. The latter does not analyze an objective phenomenon called Christianity simply in order to unveil it further. He rather seeks to reflect on the historical phenomenon of Christianity, or the tradition as we would call it, in order to move from the phenomenon itself to its real ontology, that is, to move from *dasein* to *sein*, from *existence* to *être*. This is essentially the same quest upon which Heidegger embarked and which he seems to have given up along the way.

The purpose of Christian reflection is not to analyze with precise scientific tools the historical phenomenon called Christ and his Church, so that we know exactly how it was put together. Christian reflection is an opening up of oneself to the Christ and Church phenomenon, and through it to the God who manifests himself in it, just as Heidegger uses his process of *dasein*-analysis to seek access to being.

Here a totally fresh attitude is necessary, one which is different from our objectifying-analyzing technique. We shall call it the *reverent-receptive* attitude. It is the attitude of being open to fundamental reality as it manifests itself to us through visible, audible, sensible realities in the creation. This fresh attitude is not to be adopted as a alternative to the scientific-technological attitude but as a necessary complement. Without this combination the scientific-technological attitude becomes as harmful as the other attitude becomes obscurantist and self-deceiving.

Traces of this reverent-receptive attitude seem to be present in the finest scientists and philosophers of science. One of the best examples is the scientist philosopher, Michael Polanyi, the respected though difficult-to-understand agnostic.[3] In a very perceptive analysis of creative scientific discovery, he shows the important role played by passive receptivity. This amounts almost to a faith that reality will respond in a particular way, faith that is then confirmed by experience. The difficulty, however, arises from the fact that this child-like receptivity seems to be regarded as essential only for scientific discovery and not necessarily for the practice of science. Once the experiment has confirmed the expectation, the theory belongs to Karl Popper's World III of objective scientific theories which man has created and owns and can objectify for further examination in order to eliminate error and generate more problems.

The reverent-receptive attitude is exemplified in some poetry, literature, music, and art, but not in all. Many examples could be cited in poetry by Rainer Maria Rilke and Alexander Pope, Thomas Traherne and Rabindranath Tagore, T. S. Eliot and John Donne, Blake and Goethe, Gerard Manley Hopkins and Raissa Maritain, as well as many others in all climes and cultures.

A deeper level of this same reverent-receptive attitude is found in true prayer — not prayer as another manipulative technique to control reality, but as self-surrender and receptivity, prayer in which repentance and self-emptying are followed by self-dedication and a willingness to be molded anew by the gladdening light. Not prayer as petition or even intercession, not prayer for oneself, nor for some other utilitarian purpose, but prayer as described by Richard Crashaw:

> Lord, when the sense of thy sweet grace
> Sends up my soul to seek thy face,
> Thy blessed eyes breed such desire,
> I die in love's delicious fire.

Such prayer is the communication of love with the Truly Other of all creation, the fulfillment of creation by surrender to the loving arms of the creator.

Our civilization renders us increasingly incapable of such prayer. And until it becomes once again a possibility for us, all the pollution prevention, recycling of resources, decentralization of urban conglomerations, population control, creation of new energy sources, reshaping of our giant technology into a more manageable, more human, middle technology, shifting from an exclusive to an inclusive understanding of nature, even the creation of a just international society—none of these can assure the fulfillment for which we ardently long.

Science and technology have so alienated us from reality that only two possibilities are open to us: to stand apart from it and know it objectively, or to manipulate it technologically. We have become so accustomed to the scientific-technological stance that we have lost the faculty of addressing reality as a whole, of seeing in it the source and sustainer of life, of responding to it with reverence and receptivity, and of surrendering ourselves to it in all-fulfilling love. We have lost the capacity to respond with our whole being to the being of the Wholly Other who presents himself to us through the created universe.

Here a word of caution is needed. Perceptive philosophers of science have pointed out that science itself is holistic in that it seeks to find a clear, simple unity in reality as it presents itself to us. J. Bronowski, for example, tells us that science is a base for the sense of being at one with nature, because the very objective of science is to seek a conceptually-unified picture of the organic and inorganic universe expressed through mathematical continuum informed by universal law. It is true that in science there is a search for unity, but as we have shown, this is a reduced unity, a unity within our knowledge and control, not one to which we surrender, but one which we objectify and manipulate. The ultimate aim of science may be to explain all things in terms of a single set of laws. But we are not concerned here with explaining reality as a whole, but with relating ourselves—the *pleroma* of humanity—to it, not in an intellectual-operational, self-reductive, individualistic way, but in a personal, self-fulfilling, total, communitarian way. Nor are we talking about some mystic flight of the mind seeking rhapsodic union of the "alone with the lone". Here we must express our dissent from most of the Indo-Hellenic cosmologies which seek fulfillment and personal unity with a Transcendent Absolute through rejecting as illusion the world of matter, nature, and history. The way of thought of Sankara, the great Indian sage, is typical of what we are *not* advocating. We seek not a mystical union divorced from the reality of time and history, but a genuine Christ mysticism of the Pauline-Johannine type. We cannot, therefore, accept either the Old Gnosis which Theodore Roszak advocates or the "return to nature" which many romanticists recommend.

Mysticism is an ugly word in Western thought, half understood, often fascinating. Calvinism held it under strong taboo, as neo-Calvinists like Emile Brunner have shown. They fear that the mystic quest is an affront to the unique mediatorship of Christ, since in the mystics' accounts of their experience they always speak of unmediated union with God. Harnack thought that together mystery and dogma constituted the twin distortions of pure Christianity by the Hellenic spirit. We shall therefore seek to avoid the word "mysticism" and plead for participatory union, in and with Christ, with the *energeia* of God as it gives existence to us and to all other reality in creation.

This union with God and with each other in Christ is the true meaning of the eucharist, and the only authentically Christian mysticism. This eucharistic union-mysticism, in which we are one with the whole creation in our responsive self-offering to God, is the mystery that fulfills human existence. As Paul Evdokimov puts it:

> The word by which the eucharist was instituted, 'this is my body', designates the living body, the whole Christ conferring on every communicant a quickening consanguinity and concorporality. In the same way, 'the word was made flesh', means that God has assumed human nature in its entirety and in it, the whole cosmos. And the 'resurrection of the flesh' in the Creed confesses the reconstitution of the whole man, soul and body; and thus 'all flesh shall see the salvation of God', all flesh meaning the pleroma of nature.[4]

"Sacrament" is not a didactic reduction of the "word", a *verbum visibile*, as Augustine put it. The Greek word "mystery" used by Eastern Christians for the eucharist has two connotations: one, being initiated into the heavenly choir surrounding the presence of God; the other, an act of love between God and his universe through the mediation of man in Christ. The two are linked. Initiation implies participation, and true participation is love, a mutual perochoresis in which God and the universe embrace and penetrate each other.

In a sense, this is why marriage is sacrament or mystery: not because through it grace is given, but because the marriage relationship at its best is the reflection and sacrament of this mutual self-giving, this mutual embracing and interpenetration of God and the universe of love.

When the objectifying and alienating technological relationship of humanity to nature is overemphasized, humanity loses the capacity for this self-giving mutual love between God and the universe, this love which constitutes human nature. We are fast losing this capacity for self-giving. This loss to our proper humanity caused by our technological civilization is greater than all the harm it has done through pollution, resource depletion, and all the rest.

In our relation to nature, we have to walk the precarious path and live in the difficult rhythm between mystery and mastery. It is not technology and theology or science and theology that need to be reconciled. It is rather these two attitudes — mastery and mystery — which have to be held in tension. Our mastery of the universe is like the mastery of our bodies; it is not that we may have it for our own use, but that we may give nature, as our extended body, into the hands of the loving God in the great mystery of the eucharistic self-offering. This is the mystery of the cross. Christ gave himself, with humanity and nature, to God, in self-denying love, and thereby saved humanity and nature. It is in that eternal act of sacrifice and love that we too are called upon to participate. Technology is the way of humanizing the world of matter in time-space, and thereby of extending the human body to envelop the whole universe. But that humanizing and extension, if it is to be salvific, must find its proper culmination in man's offering of himself and the universe to God in love. A secular technology of mastery of nature for oneself is the "original" sin, of refusing our mediatory position between God and the universe, dethroning God, and claiming mastery for the sake of indulging our own cupidity, avarice, and greed.

The mastery of nature must be held within the mystery of worship. Otherwise we lose both mastery and mystery.

CHAPTER EIGHT

Iconopeia: The Art of Making Images of the Future

The science of the future is originally a Marxist doctrine. Marxism, as an eschatological sociology, had ascribed the status of scientific knowledge to the concept of a freely fabricated utopia drawn from elements of 19th-century Western Europe, the Old Testament, and the human imagination. Yet in the past four decades, a science of the future has been spreading in liberal thought also, and has become a "science in the making" in the West.[1] The terminology, however, has not been fully agreed upon: some speak of *futurology*, others of *futuristics*, yet others of *prognostics*.

Human Futuristics, as Professor Magoroh Maruyama points out,[2] cannot be just another branch of science in the traditional sense. It does not analyze an object in the external world given to us now; it cannot make predictions about the future because human goals are involved and people's intentions, imagination, and willpower cannot be accurately measured or predicted. They vary from time to time, from person to person.

Futuristics is in some sense science, in another sense engineering, and in yet another sense philosophy, and, why not, in some instances prophecy. The advocates of futuristics disclaim all utopianism. They claim a scientific basis for their prognostications. But they are concerned also with helping in the process of articulating social goals, and to that extent they are engaged in a form of human engineering.

95

When it comes to the question of methodology in the study of the future, however, one has to turn philosopher and ask questions which cannot be answered by science or engineering. One of these questions refers to the perennial problem of conceptualizing time. Man is constantly living in a fleeting and moving moment of time, the point of intersection between the past and the future. Definition of time itself seems therefore to be impossible.

The future is an aspect of that time, yet it is so different from that other dimension of time, namely the past. The past is gone by but has left its carcass; we can investigate its remains and recapture a vision of it. It is precisely because the past is dead that we can study it with our palaeontological, archaeological, or historical tools.

It is not simply the capacity to conceptualize time that we lack. Polak claims that modern Western man has lost the necessary human capacity to conceive images of future time and to move towards them.[3] According to him, man had always done both — projecting the *ideal* future as it ought to be and working out the *real* future through goal-oriented action in history.

Polak argues that irrational tools have been more influential than scientific thinking in bringing about renewal of the vision of the future:

> The very concept of the future inhabits another world to which experience has no access. Neither does pure reason, if such a thing exists. Thinking about the future requires faith and visionary powers, mixed with philosophic detachment, a rich emotional life and creative fantasy.[4]

There can be little doubt that we are in a time when the prophetic task is not one of destructive criticism of a decadent system, but rather of engaging in the creative art of image making or *iconopeia*. How are images made? Who makes them? What kind of images of the future do we need? How can they be communicated? These are the pressing questions which immediately arise.

Polak insists that the origin of these images is always *aristocratic*. Images of the future cannot be mass-produced or produced by the masses. In fact, their acceptance by the masses is never achieved without struggle and resistance. The demolition of old images and their replacement by new ones is therefore a process which usually takes place only over a long period of time.

But can images of the future be freely fabricated without reference to the past and only in relation to the present? There is a persistent illusion that the past can be left alone, and projections for the future can be done solely on the basis of the present. The data and determinants to be chosen and used for creating an effective and sane image of the future are so vast that most savants lose all hope of mastering the information. Scientific data, philosophical skill, and faith are all necessary equipment for image making, but under scientific data we must include also knowledge of the past — history, anthropology, palaeontology, and the life sciences. Perhaps we need to know also something about the history of religion, about magic and ritual, myth and mystery, and occult and the revealed. Image making calls for a measure of direct experience of the transcendent. Without some asceticism and mystical experience, intuition and ecstasy, genuine practice of the art of *iconopeia* is virtually impossible. This is perhaps one of the besetting faults of many modern prognostications of the future which are purely ideological-rational. Computers cannot create effective icons of the future.

Olivier Reiser, whose earlier work was praised by Albert Einstein, Aldous Huxley, and John Dewey, is one who has brought a lucid mind and an encyclopaedic knowledge of science, religion, and art to the task of making images of the future. In his *Cosmic Humanism*,[5] he learnedly advances the hypothesis that "men are the embryonic cells (neuroblasts) of an emerging world organism;. . .we are participating in the embryogenesis of a giant organism".[6] In a manner reminiscent of Teilhard de Chardin but also refreshingly free from Christian symbols, Reiser reconstructs the ladder of ascent by which evolution has moved from elementary particles through atoms, molecules, cells, unicellular organisms, and multicellular organisms to achieve the level of complexity-intensity called the individual man. His suggestion is that man's social organization and intercommunication is simply the next higher level of cosmic evolution which, by the free volition of humanity, must constitute a planet-wide human race interconnected by all forms of communication, which will then serve as a "world sensorium", a kind of brain of the earth. He conceives the planet earth as a psychosomatic creature, with an organized humanity forming its brain cortex.

But the intercommunication between all parts of humanity cannot be merely a verbal affair. Reiser proposes a world-level picture language, and a planet-wide communication medium using an artificial sea of electricity "enveloping the globe in the near-vacuum hundreds of miles above the earth's surface". This would not be simply a sort of mirror transmitter for ordinary television communication in time and space which cannot go faster than the speed of light. Reiser, as a scientist, is bold enough to predict the possibility of communication via sub-ether influences at a velocity approximating infinity",[7] that is the kind of communication which requires no time lapse or physical signals.

Reiser's eight-dimensional cosmos includes the four-dimensional universe of our sense perception which he calls the *manifest universe*. But science itself has come to the conclusion that the manifest universe cannot be understood in itself. Recent discoveries in physics about particle-antiparticle symmetry lend force to the conjecture of an *unmanifest* universe, parallel to the manifest one. Reiser's hypothesis is not in terms of an antiuniverse but of a universe, unmanifest, not obeying the laws of time and space and the unsurpassibility of the speed of light, related to and impinging upon the manifest universe at every point. Reiser cites Freeman Dyson:

> Nature has a double-layer structure. In the lower layer, there exist electric and magnetic fields, which satisfy simple wave equations and travel freely through space in the form of light or radio waves. In the upper layer, there are material objects, energies and forces. Only the upper layer is directly accessible to our observation. A lower-layer object, such as an electric field, can only be observed by looking at the energies and forces it produces in the upper layer.[8]

The discovery of quantum fields and plasma physics has only added to the complexity of our picture of the universe and its inaccessibility to the ordinary mind. But even ordinary people can alter their usual static picture of the world, to that of a flowing, moving, directed process, an un-uniform process with quantum jumps, but a process with a goal. While we can thus picture a four-dimensional image of the cosmos accessible to our observation, what is the nature of the dimensions which we are still missing?

The major difficulty with the Whiteheadian or Teilhardian images of the universe is at this point. Our known sciences have access to one of the two poles of the universe — the time-space continuum with sense-objects — but not to the other pole where the laws of time and space and the subject-object dichotomy in knowledge may not directly apply. We have occasional glimpses into this other universe through the strange phenomena now fairly well attested by experiments in what are called parapsychology, psychokinesis, clairvoyance, telepathy, and extrasensory perception. Until yesterday, these phenomena were taboos to science. In an article in the *New York Times*[9] ex-astronaut Edgar D. Mitchell, who is now president of the Institute of Noetic Sciences in Palo Alto, makes his confession of how his own experiments in outer space converted him from scepticism to conviction about extrasensory perception. What is more important, Mitchell clearly states that "the evidence of psychic research suggests that awareness can operate externally to the body and that therefore it is not unreasonable to hypothesize that mind may be able to operate independently of the body". With appropriate scientific modesty he concludes:

> Whether or not the survival question is answered, psychic research has already put us in a position where it appears that science's basic concept of man and the universe must be revised to some degree.[10]

As Christians we are not concerned primarily about survival, either personal or collective. Out central interest is in discerning the signs of the times, in order to be prepared for *iconopeia*, that subtle art of creating images which are in conformity with both our possibilities and our own vocation as human beings. *Iconopeia*, however, will remain an ever incomplete attempt, since whatever images we make of the future, there is every likelihood that we will miss out certain vital dimensions which are as yet unknown to us. But it is part of human growth, and an expression of our genuine *Mündigkeit* as humanity, to recognize the existence of these immense layers of reality which have hitherto been insufficiently grasped by our approved scientific methods. The fact that our scientific theories are unable to account for phenomena like those reported in Carlos Castaneda's *The Teachings of Don Juan*[11] should not lead us to discredit the reports, but rather push us to explore further the limits of our scientific or publicly-certified knowledge. A helpful compilation of such areas of further exploration has been provided by Professor Lawrence Foss in a very perceptive article, entitled, "Does Don Juan Really Fly?"[12] His list includes: dreams as revelations; relation between stars and man; psychic phenomena; the dead; the knowledge that I has of Thou; the universe as alive; space as a manifold of localities with emotional color; gods; the way things experience us; chimeras; knowledge acquisition as a matter of "emptying the contents of consciousness", and *déjà vu* experiences.[13]

Ceylonese firewalking is now a well-attested phenomenon, and cannot be dismissed as collective hallucination. According to Feinberg's report, for example, 12 people failed to achieve firewalking without injury and had to be hospitalized, and one was burned to death, but 68 others managed to walk on live coals barefoot without injury.[14]

The present writer comes from a culture where such phenomena are still widely observable, because not all the people have been reduced to the single vision of the scientific mentality. Professor Foss's remarks are well worth heeding:

> Perhaps in this respect a problem of western man is that he has yet to achieve a 'critique of the self', systematically to probe the possibility that true knowledge (*scientia*) is achieved through 'becoming whole', through release from the 'I-ness' of the ego-consciousness in favour of the inward (godlike) man. So thoroughgoing has been our 'extroversion' that 'technology' comes to be identified with applications only of the *askesis* of science, conceivably blinding us to '. . . perceptual solicitations of a world outside the descriptions we have learned to call reality. . .' Is it possible that our beliefs restructure the way we shape our data, that the light in the clearing (intellectual light) determines what is seen in the dark beyond?[15]

The point worth heeding is the possibility that our whole culture, our whole educational system, our schools, colleges, universities, libraries, and laboratories are training us to be transcendent-vision-blind. Science is not as objective a system of knowledge as we once thought it was. It is an option that we have chosen and which has given birth to the impressive reality of Western scientific-technological, urban-industrial civilization. We are part of that system: it is our creation. We have chosen to limit our perception to the scientifically explicable, and despite the challenge of many phenomena which could have told us that there is something fundamentally wrong with the system, we have gone ahead, hoping that all mysteries can be reduced to problems and puzzles soluble by intelligent conceptual investigation.

Here is the true problem of futuristics. Are we going to project the future entirely and exclusively in terms of the limited possibilities of our science and technology, or are we prepared to conceive a future in which the full potentiality of human existence is taken into account? Are Christians not to have an understanding of the meaning of existence that shatters the fetters of time and death, and liberates us to envision and to create a future that is more than the product of scientific-technological creativity?

CHAPTER NINE

Towards a New Style
of Christian Ethical Reflection

1. APPROACHES TO QUESTIONS OF CLASSICAL ETHICS

There are two fundamental questions of classical ethics, namely: What is the good that I should do?; and Why should I do good? The first question relates to *norms* and the second to rationale. The two are obviously interrelated and inseparable.

There are two possible approaches to answering these questions. One is to develop answers on a contextual and pragmatic basis, irrespective of all ontological questions, and without reference to any total understanding of the nature of reality as a whole. Even here, it is impossible to avoid totally the concept of norms or principles; one has to adduce some category like the dominical command to love one's neighbor as oneself or the secular norm of humaneness. Matters are further complicated by the fact that it is possible to arrive at practically the same decisions about the course of action to be taken whether one starts from the dominical command or the secular principle.

Western humanism is the creation of an interaction between the values of classical Greece and those of Western Christendom. These values themselves were once grounded in an ontology, a total picture of reality developed in the experience and reflection of classical Greece and in the Judaeo-Christian tradition. Consequently, in order to criticize and assess these values, it is necessary to see their integral relation to ancient world-views and to examine the extent to which these could be integral to our own world-view. This examination and evaluation of world-views can be regarded as the main task of what is called ontology or metaphysics. It therefore seems impossible for some of us in the Eastern tradition to ignore ontology and metaphysics, and simply to accept a principle or norm by—what appears to us—an arbitrary choice.

Take two examples: the Universal Declaration of Human Rights (UDHR), and the recently raised issues about the rights of future generations, yet unborn, or even of subhuman nature.

The preamble of the UDHR seeks to indicate the basis of fundamental "human rights":

1.   Recognition of the inherent dignity and of the equal and inalienable rights of all members of the human family is the foundation of freedom, justice, and peace in the world.

2.   Disregard and contempt for human rights have resulted in barbarous acts which have outraged the conscience of mankind.

3.   The advent of a world in which human beings shall enjoy freedom of speech and belief and freedom from fear and want has been proclaimed as the highest aspiration of the common people.

4.   The peoples of the United Nations have in the Charter reaffirmed their faith in fundamental human rights, in the dignity and worth of the human person, and in the equal rights of men and women, and have determined to promote social progress and better standards of life in larger freedom.

A careful examination of these statements gives rise to many questions. On what ground, for example, can we refer to a human family, when there are only nations warring against each other? On what basis do we affirm the *equal* rights of all? What do we mean by the "conscience of mankind", by "the dignity and worth of the human person", etc.? It becomes clear that it is only on the basis of a consensus coming out of totally different conceptions of reality that this common faith is arrived at.

The idea of the rights of future generations yet unborn and of subhuman nature is even more problematic. What exactly is meant by "right"? Is it a right adjudicable before a court of law? Can the human conscience alone be sufficient ground for defining rights? Or shall we press for legislation defining rights on the basis of expediency? Expediency is clearly the most immediately attractive motivation for most human beings. But are Christians justified in asking for legislation and enforcement purely on this basis?

While the value of the concept of rights as legally negotiable terms needs to be recognized, it is important to emphasize that, ultimately, the Christian Church cannot depend for its definition of rights on law and legal enforcement. Christians can speak about rights only on the basis of a prior understanding of the particular origin of things in God. Equally, when, owing to circumstances, our understanding of particular rights becomes questionable, there is no way to correct ourselves except by going back to the ontological roots of these rights.

Another problem regarding rights is that the concept seems to operate in an individualistic framework. The Universal declaration of Human Rights itself, being essentially a product of Western liberalism, provides a striking example of this problem. It speaks only about the rights and freedoms of individuals. The words "everyone", "no one", occur like a chorus in each of the articles. There is no mention of freedom of humanity. The freedom of each nation from internal or external exploitation is barely touched upon. Education (art. 26:2) is oriented towards "the full development of the human personality". Only as an afterthought, in the last two articles (28 and 29), does UDHR declare that "everyone is entitled to a social and international order in which the rights and freedoms set forth in this declaration can be fully realized", and that "everyone has duties to the community".

It is this individualistic framework within which the concept of rights generally operates that makes it problematic for the Eastern Orthodox thinker who has to derive his ethics from his ontology despite dogmatic prohibitions about deriving an ought from an is. The Eastern Christian does not derive his norm from canon law or other ethical legislation by official church bodies. The general axiom is rather that the full-grown human being, the saint, is free from all laws in the Church. Human freedom is too important for Eastern spirituality to be made subordinate to any kind of law, whether of Church or state. People are meant to be kings — not obedient servants. They are not slaves in the house of God: he is a son of God, she is a daughter.[1]

There is no other norm for the good than God himself as known and understood by us. This is a dynamic norm, because God is dynamic, his will is dynamic, the universe is dynamic, and our understanding of all three is changing. In God's economy, the norm for the good cannot be captured in words. It can only be embodied and lived. And then the horizon is infinitely receding. Every formal norm is thus open to revision as God moves us on in history and makes us see new and surprising aspects of his wisdom and power.

The norm for the good is God, and the rationale for doing the good is that God who is good alone is worthy of love, and that in doing what is good we express our love of God. We cannot, as Christians, separate ethics from an ontology based on our partial knowledge of the universe and our partial knowledge of God's plan and purpose. Precisely because both are partial, every ontology will remain provisional and open to constant revision. Only such ontologically-based ethical reflection can engage the attention and interest of Eastern Orthodox thinkers.

2. THE QUESTION OF PRIORITIES

While ethical decisions must be made in the wider context of human existence in divine economy, the Eastern Orthodox thinker is not totally unconcerned with questions of strategy and expediency. As already outlined above,[2] three major problems need to be faced by humanity today: (a) the appalling poverty of billions of people, perpetuated by atrocious economic injustice and exploitation; (b) satiety, boredom, and a sense of meaninglessness among the affluent, raising fundamental questions about the values of the consumer society and the urban industrial civilization based on it; and (c) fundamental challenges to the human future posed by the cumulative perils of a scientific-technological culture, such as resource depletion, pollution, and the possibilities of misuse of artificial gene mutation, not to mention nuclear war.

Where should the priority be put? There is no doubt that the problems of world poverty and injustice cannot wait. Is the solution then a strategy for simultaneous de-development of the affluent and accelerated development of the poor? No economist seems so far to have provided a convincing and workable formula for such economic changes, and the poor of the world have very little reason to count upon the goodwill of the affluent, for such goodwill has never existed in the structures of Western society. Some young counter-culturists may willingly choose nonaffluence and preach persuasively their way of life, but it is unrealistic to hope that the transition from a consumer society to a new, simple, spontaneous, nontechnocratic society will be brought about by persuasion and gradual changes.

Yet if we as Christians and as part of humanity are to seize the *kairos* that is facing us, we must use the technological-ecological crisis to devise and practice a new way of life. We have to create a new pattern of civilization wherein humanity can grow towards the fullness of its God-given vocation. No blueprint for such a way of life can be given in advance. It will have to be worked out experimentally, in actual practice, within experimental communities with built-in feedback mechanisms.

Experimental communities cannot, however, solve the problems of humanity. Simple living in spontaneous communities, divorced from the concern for structures of universal justice, is no way to the future. The way will be found only through political, economic, and social decision undertaken by humanity as a whole. This is where the concern for justice and the concern for the environment should converge.

Only a new civilization and a new world grid of economic and political power can lead humanity forward. As the values of our civilization change from acquisitiveness and aggressiveness combined with parochial, national, or racial loyalties, we can hope to develop the right kind of world grid of power. The term "grid" emphasizes the longitudinal and latitudinal distribution of power: this distribution must be equitable both within and between sociopolitical units in world society. But efforts to develop such a grid within a capitalistic-acquisitive economy, or even in a mixed economy as conceived of by the World Council of Churches in its idea of a "responsible society", seem self-contradictory and self-defeating. Unless the values change, justice cannot be achieved.

Values, however, cannot be changed without changing the dominant systems. The holders of power in the present systems, obviously eager to maintain their position, will allow only slight and peripheral changes. They can mitigate the exploitation by occasional gifts, aid packets, and loans. They can create both state and private institutions of charity which help the poor of the world whom they are constantly exploiting. Often the churches stand ready to contribute to this mitigating and hiding of the exploitative character of the prevailing systems by becoming the instruments of those systems, either through the benign and "Christian" act of distributing aid or in other ways.

They manage to hide their own role as defenders of these systems by occasionally indulging in verbal criticism of them. If the critics of these opressive systems go so far as to give token assistance to those struggling for liberation or raise issues that touch the heart of the economic structures, for example, the nature of capitalist investment, then they are vehemently repudiated by many within the churches.

The churches' participation in an exploitative capitalist system and the benefits they derive from that system would thus seem to be a primary target in any sincere attempt to change the system in the direction of justice for all humanity. A corresponding challenge is posed to churches living in other contemporary systems which have their own forms of oppression.

3. TOWARDS A NEW SPIRITUALITY IN COMMUNITY

It is obvious that Christian reflection cannot take place only in the minds of individual Christians. No one human being is capable of bringing together the vast insights of human culture and the Christian tradition. How then can we bring about a new style of life, a new design for living, working, creating, producing, relating ourselves to reality in all its aspects? Can such a design for living, which incorporates a new spirituality, be worked out theoretically before we actually experiment with it?

There is today an urgent need for an interdisciplinary, intercultural, interreligious community of mature, capable, charismatic people who will live together for five to ten years in a place where, despite the difference of nationalities, they can:

a)   participate fully in the life and struggles of the community around them, taking an active role in the political, social, religious, and cultural life of the people;

b)   evolve a way of life, a style of living in community, with simplicity and spontaneity, not averse to productive manual labor, not closed to the world outside, not afraid of poverty (preferably in the midst of a nonaffluent society), not closed to the religious and cultural sensitivities of others in the community at large;

c)   engage in serious and informed study and reflection on the problems that confront humanity today, projecting its future to the extent possible; such reflection to lead to the creation of patterns of living, producing, and educating which can be copied by the world outside;

d) embody a new spirituality-*askesis*, based on prayer, meditation, worship, and sacramental life; on loving service and unostentatious self-sacrifice; on humility and graciousness; on overcoming acquisitiveness and aggressiveness; on transparency to each other and to the transcendent.

We can list here only a few of the areas to which such a participating-reflecting community of charismatic persons would need to give particular attention:

a) Freedom from attachment to property.

Property is a fundamentally dehumanizing way by which man relates himself to external reality. From childhood on, the desire to possess things as "mine" as distinct from those which are "thine" and the establishment of a realm of domination called private property are fostered in our culture. Property is regarded as necessary for establishing individual identity. Can we experiment with alternate ways of affirming personal identity in terms of what one *is* rather than what one *has*? Should there not be limits even for "common property" of the community? Can the community also be delivered from such attachment? May it not need to establish a relationship to the means of production other than that of ownership? This would apply to the land, the buildings in which the community lives and carries on its activity, and all equipment.

Total poverty can be only a partial answer. We are searching for a community which sets models for society at large and which needs to have some—quite limited—means of production, distribution, communication, etc.

b) Limits to privacy.

Privacy is intimately linked to private property, and has even become a fundamental right in our individualistic property-oriented civilization. A certain measure of privacy seems to be necessary for the conservation and development of personal identity, inwardness, and creativity. But have we not made a cult of privacy, regarding it somehow as an integral part of personal freedom itself. Is it absolutely necessary to keep a private realm free from external incursion, say for meditation and prayer? Jesus and Gandhi seemed to need such privacy. Both had a long period of it in preparation for the public ministry, as well as regular short periods of private prayer — in Jesus' case often all night, in Gandhi's for several hours in the night and early morning. But for both that privacy was replenished by love of and contacts with the masses. When they were not praying, their whole being, all their spiritual energy, was unstintingly at the disposal of the masses. The community would thus have to work out a design which:

i)   would ensure that its members did not get their spiritual training in isolation from the masses and in alienation from social reality;

ii)   would protect its members from over-exposure to the public;

iii)   would make possible a discipline of worship, love, and community through which the human person could grow inwardly.

Only such privacy as would be necessary for these ends would need to be developed.

c) *Productive activity.*

The community would have to be actively engaged in production — agricultural (primary), industrial (secondary), and diaconal (tertiary, that is, services in such areas as health, education, welfare, communication, art, music, research, etc.). But such production should be guided by the following considerations:

i)   the basic orientation of all production should be to serve others and not to accumulate profits;

ii)   the productive activity should be shared by all members of the community, but no member should be required to spend more than four hours per day in economic production, in order not to give it undue importance;

iii)   the technology used should be nonalienating, that is, the machine should not become a tyrant that makes people do *its* will;

it should be kind to nature, nonpolluting, resource-conserving, and moderate in size and in the number of people attached to each unit. It should be adapted to the society within which the community lives. If the community has large numbers of unemployed the technology should be such as to permit maximum use of human labor, and so on.

d)   Major emphasis on diaconal activity.

The community would need to design new ways of educating people; new ways of caring for their health; new art, literature, and music related to the problems of humanity; new and inexpensive professional services (lawyers' services, insurance, house construction, etc.) easily accessible to the poor of the community. The community would also engage in research on the structures of exploitation and injustice in society, fearlessly exposing evil and conscientizing and politicizing people to fight against such evils and to restructure a more just and humane society.

Christians could take the initiative in creating such a community, which should be open to others. The community should include a wide range of competences and cultures. It should be possible to organize subcommunities within the larger community, so that different religious traditions could be embodied and lived out in a context of openness to others. Maximum variety with maximum community should be the principle.

From such a community, new reflection and new patterns of living may emerge which could have a prophetic role in the world. For it is the *energeia* of God in Christ that should be available to us as both existence and grace, as we conscientiously seek to follow him, the captain of our salvation who has gone before us.

Postscript

The purpose of this book is to make two pleas—one for an intellectual renewal that will correct our world picture; the other for a genuine international community effort to face some of the ethical problems confronting humanity.

The primary intellectual error is the failure to take account of the reality of God in our picture of reality. This is the practical atheism that pervades our cultures today. The secondary error is that in our mental picture which is composed of only two realities—self and world—we go wrong again by assuming towards the world the subject-object attitude and the instrumental attitude so characteristic of our kind of science and technology. The plea, therefore, is that we recover the more adequate reality-conception—with God as fundamental reality, and with the world as the second reality, to be shaped by the mediating third called humanity, which participated in the reality of both God and the world.

Such an integral and mediatory view of humanity has implications not only for Christian theology or philosophy, but also for our economics, our cultural constructions, and even for our politics. These implications are not worked out here. The author lacks the competence for that.

All that is presented here is a second plea: that there be a community effort for production and distribution based on these new ethical and ontological insights. Such a community should be a pioneering and model-making one, so that its values can gradually be assimilated by society at large.

There is here no naive assumption that this process of assimilation would be smooth and unruffled. Conflict is inevitable where the interests of the beneficiaries of injustice are threatened. Justice in a dynamic form should be part of any such community experiment. And the effort towards justice always plants the cross of conflict in the midst of our sin-mixed history.

Notes

CHAPTER ONE

1. "Brookhaven Biology Symposium, 1969," cited in John B. Cobb, Jr., *Is It Too Late? A Theology of Ecology* (New York: Bruce Publishing Company, 1972), p. 13.
2. Ibid.
3. Fred Polak puts it this way: "The challenge of our future waits, none too patiently, at our very door. If we do not hasten to answer it, we may lose both our freedom to give an answer, and our future too. The future can be a hostile mother, devouring her weak and sickly offspring. In that case, visions and future alike might perish." *The Image of the Future*, Vol. I. (Leyden: Sythoff; New York: Oceana Publications, 1961), p. 53.
4. Donella H. Meadows, Denis H. Meadows, Jörgen Randers, and William W. Behrens III: *The Limits to Growth: A Report for the Club of Rome's Project on the Predicament of Mankind* (New York: Universe Books, 1972).
5. Professor Alfred Sauvy of the Collège de France has reminded us that the desire to keep population stationary is as old as Plato and Aristotle. See *Croissance zéro?* (Paris: Calmann-Levy, 1973). Plato in *The Laws* suggests fixing the number of citizens in the ideal city at 5,040, which meant a population of around 20-25,000, including the slaves. The advantage of the number 5,040 is that it is divisible without remainder by the first 10 integers, and so lends well to subgrouping!
6. In his study, *Croissance zéro?*, op. cit., p. 167, Professor Sauvy regards American alarmism as a psychosis, a national mental disorder without much relation to reality. One cannot but partly agree with him. The language in which the threat is posed by writers like Paul Ehrlich does not increase the credibility of their message.
7. Cited in Michael Hamilton, (ed.), *This Little Planet* (New York: Charles Scribner's Sons, 1970), p. 42.
8. In *Science* (Vol. 155, 10 March, 1967): 1203-1207.
9. R. W. Southern presents a fascinating analysis in which even medieval monasticism is seen as aggressively expansionist and greedy. See *Western Society and the Church in the Middle Ages: Pelican History of the Church*, Vol. III (Harmondsworth: Penguin, 1972).
10. Conrad Bonifazi, "Biblical Roots of an Ecological Conscience" in *This Little Planet*, op. cit., p. 205.

CHAPTER TWO

1. "A Problem for Theology: The Concept of Nature" in *Harvard Theological Review* (No. 65, July 1972):337-366.
2. Frederick Elder, *Crisis in Eden: A Religious Study of Man and Environment* (Nashville: Abingdon, 1970).
3. For a fuller discussion of the meanings of the word, see R. G. Collingwood, *The Idea of Nature* (New York: Oxford, 1945); or C. F. von Weizäcker, *The History of Nature* (Chicago: University of Chicago Press, 1959); or in a briefer framework, Gordon Kaufman, "A Problem for Theology," op. cit.
4. Hatch and Redpath, *Concordance to the Septuagint* (Oxford: Clarendon Press, 1897). This work gives the following instances: Wisdom 7:1; 13:1; 19:20; III Maccabees 3:29; IV Maccabees 1:20; 5:7,8,25; 13:27; 15:13,25, and 16: 3.
5. It should be remembered not only that the Old Testament has no word for nature (inclusive or exclusive), but that it has no word for what we call the "universe". The closest it comes to this is "heaven and earth". The word *olam*, which many writers view as an Old Testament concept for the universe, does not occur very frequently. In ninety-nine percent of the cases, it is used to mean "forever", "everlastingly", rather than the "world". The closest equivalent to an inclusive sense of nature in the Hebrew Scriptures is *tebel*—the inhabited or "hominized" earth— parallel to the Greek *oikumene*.
6. IV Maccabees 5:5-8, Eng. tr. R. H. Charles, *The Apocrypha and Pseudepigrapha of the Old Testament in English*, Vol. II (Oxford: Clarendon Press, 1913), p. 672.
7. ὁ δ' οὐρανὸς ἔμψυχος καὶ ἔχει κινήσεως ἀρχὴν Aristotle: *De Caelo* B 2, 285, a 29-30. See also *De Gen. Anim.* B 6, 744 b 16-17; *De Caelo* Bs, 288, a 2.
8. ὁ δὲ Θεὸς καὶ ἡ φύσις οὐδὲν μάτην ποιοῦσιν was a common dictum to which Aristotle refers in *De Caelo*.
9. *Katha* V:9-12. Eng. tr. Radhakrishnan and Moore (eds.), *A Source Book in Indian Philosophy* (Bombay: Princeton & Oxford University Press, 1957).
10. *Katha* V:12.
11. *A Source Book in Indian Philosophy*, op. cit., p. 139.
12. S. S. Suryanarayana Sastri (ed. and tr.), *The Samkhyakarika of Isvarakrishna* (Madras:1935). See also *A Source Book in Indian Philosophy*, op. cit, pp. 424-452.
13. It is possible to give here only a sampling of the Patristic literature on the subject of nature, and the furious debates about Christ's nature which led to the unfortunate and unproductive schism of the Church in the 5th and 6th centuries will be almost completely omitted.
14. *Contra Celsum* 4, 38 PG 11:1089B.
15. *De Oratione* 27, PG 11:513A.
16. E.g., *Life of Moses*, PG 44:376D.
17. See *Opusculum* 2, 83 PG 65:1104A: τρεῖς εἰσι νοητοὶ τόποι εἰς οὓς ὁ νοῦς ἐκ μεταβολὰς εἰσέρχεται κατὰ φύσιν, παρὰ φύσιν, ὑπὲρ φύσιν.
18. *Oratio* 21, PG 6:853B.
19. See *anathema* 6 in A. Hahn (ed.), *Bibliothek der Symbole und Glaubensregeln der Alten Kirche*, 2nd ed. by L. Hahn (Breslau: Verlag Von E. Morgenstern, 1877).
20. St. Basil: *Adv. Eunomium* Bk I:12 ff., PG 29; 540C-541C; St. Gregory: *Contra Eunomium* 8. Jaeger (ed.), Vol. II: pp. 202-229 ff. PG 45:800B.
21. *De Fide Orthodoxa* 3, 4 PG 94:997A.
22. «φύσις... καὶ οὐσία ταὐτὸν ἐστιν... καὶ πάντες... οἱ τῆς ἀληθινῆς πίστεως

ὁμολογηταὶ τοῦτο γινώσκουσιν», *Capita Apologiae*, PG 86:1957A. (*Physis* and *ousia* are the same, and all who confess the true faith know this.)
23. *Praeparatio Evangelica* II:9, E. H. Gifford (ed.) (Oxford: 1903), p. 524A. PG 21:9868D.
24. *De Anima et Resurrectione*, PG 46:53C.
25. Maximus, *Epist.* 15, Migne 91:545A.
26. John of Damascus, *Dialectica* 30, PG 94:589C.
27. Liddell and Scott: *Greek-English Abridged Lexicon* (Oxford: Clarendon Press-Henry Frowde, 1883), cites Empedocles, *Frag. 13*; Pythagoras according to Aristotle, *De Caelo* 268a II; Plato, *Timaeus* 28c, 30b, etc.; Aeschylus, *Prometheus Vinctus* 275, 456, etc.; *Placita Philosophorum* 2:1,7.
28. *Greek-English Abridged Lexicon*, op. cit., cites only one instance, that is in Idomeneus Historicus: Eu:415.
29. *Phaedrus* 247c, e. Plato speaks of the true being which is without color, form, or palpability. *Republic* 597d:1-3 is also about the only true being of God.
30. Athenagoras: *Legatio Pro Christianis* 23, PG 6:944B.

CHAPTER THREE

1. See Etienne Gilson, *La Philosophie au Moyen Age* (Paris: Payot, 1925), p. 11. For a full discussion of Eriugena's thought, see Franz Anton Staudenmaier, Johannes Scotus Erigena und die Wissenschaft seiner Zeit (Frankfurt: Andreäische Buchhandlung, 1834) and M. Cappuyns, *Jean Scott Erigène: Sa Vie, Son Oeuvre, Sa Pensée* (Louvain: 1933).
2. This classification comes at the very beginning (PL 122:411B ff.) of his *De Divisione Naturae* (Pastrologia Latina 122: Cols. 441-1022) which was placed on the index as being in flagrant contradiction to the more static, medieval Catholic doctrine.
3. See Migne, *Patrologia Latina* (Paris: Garnier, 1912), Vol. 122.
4. See G. Théry, Etudes dionysiennes (Paris: 1932)., p. 6; E. Jeauneau, "Introduction to Jean Scot", *Homélie sur le Prologue de Jean, Sources Chrétiennes* 151 (Paris: Editions du Cerf, 1969), pp. 25-26.
5. Etienne Gilson, *La Philosophie au Moyen Age*, second revised and enlarged edition (Paris: Payot, 1952), p. 222.
6. *Homélie de Jean Scot, Sources Chrétiennes* 151, op. cit., pp. 190 ff. PL 122:294 ff. Author's translation.
7. PG 91:11305B.
8. Etienne Gilson, L'Esprit de la Philosophie Médiévale, second edition (Paris: J. Vrin, 1944), p. 345. Author's translation.
9. Ibid., p. 346.
10. For Aquinas' views on nature, see selections from the *Summa Theologica*, published in the Library of Christian Classics, Vol. XI, *Nature and Grace* (London: SCM Press, 1954).
11. A spate of books on him have appeared in the last couple of decades, especially in the USA. His *Opera Latine* were reprinted (Naples and Florence). Some of his original works have been translated into English, e.g.: *The Heroic Frenzies*, tr. by P. O. Memmo, Jr. (Chapel Hill, North Carolina: 1964); *Expulsion of the Triumphant Beast*, A. D. Immerti (tr.) (New Brunswick, New Jersey: Rutgers University Press, 1964). For English studies on Bruno, see Dorothea W. Singer, *Giordano Bruno: His*

Life and Thought (New York: Greenwood, 1968); Sidney T. Greenberg, *The Infinite in Giordano Bruno* (New York: Octagon, 1971); Francis A. Yates, *Giordano Bruno and the Hermetic Tradition* (Chicago: University of Chicago Press, 1964); I. L. Horowitz, *The Renaissance Philosophy of Giordano Bruno* (New York: 1952); Paul-Henri Michel, *The Cosmology of Giordano Bruno* (Ithaca, New York: Cornell University Press, 1973).

12.   A. D'Abro, *The Evolution of Scientific Thought From Newton to Einstein*, second revised edition (New York: Dover, 1950), p. 353. The book is a vigorous defense of the scientific method, and treats with considerable scorn philosophers who do not know enough science!

13.   R. G. Colodney (ed.), *Paradigms and Paradoxes: The Philosophical Challenge of the Quantum Domain* (Pittsburgh: University of Pittsburgh Press, 1972).

14.   Heinz Post, "The Trouble with Quanta" in *British Journal of the Philosophy of Science*, (Vol. 24 No. 3, September 1973):277-281.

15.   Arthur Fine, "Probability and the Interpretation of Quantum Mechanics" in *British Journal of the Philosophy of Science* (Vol. 24 No. 1, March 1973):1-3.

16.   Professor of History and Inter-disciplinary Studies, California State University, Hayward.

17.   Theodore Roszak, *The Making of a Counter Culture* (Garden City, New York: Doubleday & Co., 1969).

18.   Theodore Roszak, *Where the Wasteland Ends: Politics and Transcendence in Postindustrial Society* (Garden City, New York: Doubleday & Co., 1972; Anchor books, 1973). 19.   Ibid., p. 242.

20.   Ibid., p. 426.

21.   Ibid., p. 421.

22.   Ibid.

CHAPTER FOUR

1.   A. N. Whitehead, *The Concept of Nature* (Cambridge: Cambridge University Press, 1930), p. 3.

2.   Ibid., p. 185.

3.   Ibid., p. 46. For a one-volume compendium of Whitehead, see P. A. Schilpp (ed.), *The Philosophy of Alfred North Whitehead*, The Library of Living Philosophies (New York: Tudor Publishing Co., second edition, 1951). For French readers, the best introduction to Whitehead is in Alix Parmentier, *La Philosophie de Whitehead et le Problème de Dieu*, Bibliothèque des Archives de Philosophie, nouvelle série 7 (Paris: Beauchesrie, 1968). For an attempt to relate Whitehead to the problems of science and religion as well as man and nature, see Charles Birch, *Nature and God* (Philadelphia: Westminster Press, 1965).

4.   A. N. Whitehead, *The Principles of Natural Knowledge* (Cambridge: Cambridge University Press, second edition, 1925), pp. 61 ff.

5.   A. N. Whitehead, *Science and the Modern World* (Cambridge: Cambridge University Press, 1925).

6.   Idem., *Religion in the Making* (New York: New American Library).

7.   Idem., *Process and Reality: An Essay in Cosmology* (New York: Macmillan, 1929; reprinted New York: Humanities Press, 1957; New York: Harper Torchbooks, 1960).

8.   The very title, *Process and Reality*, seems to have reference to the ruling classic

of idealist metaphysics. F. H. Bradley, *Appearance and Reality* (New York: New American Library).

9.   See *Science and the Modern World*, op. cit., pp. 142 ff.

10.   For an attempt to explain these metaphysical assumptions within the permissible limits of linguistic philosophy, see William A. Christian, *An Interpretation of Whitehead's Metaphysics* (New Haven: Yale University Press, 1959), and his article, "Some Uses of Reason," in Leclerc (ed.), *The Relevance of Whitehead*. Prof. Christian thinks that the ontological principle of creativity which plays such a central role in Whiteheadian metaphysics is simply a general statement about all entities and not another entity existing alongside others. The principle of creativity, which plays more or less the same role as substance in Aristotle's metaphysics, has been shown to be analogous to Thomas Aquinas's general principle of *esse* by David L. Schindler, "Creativity as Ultimate: Reflections on Actuality in Whitehead, Aristotle, Aquinas" in *International Philosophical Quarterly* (Vol. XIII, No. 2, June 1973). But Schindler goes on to argue that, in both Aquinas and Whitehead, while in one sense *esse*/creativity adds nothing to other things, it adds everything to all things insofar as these things/entities would be no-things or nonentities without the *esse*/creativity principle.

11.   *Process and Reality*, op. cit., p. 521.

12.   Ibid., p. 524.

13.   Ibid., p. 529.

14.   Ibid., p. 530.

15.   W. E. Hocking, "Mind and Nature" in Schilpp (ed.), *The Philosophy of Alfred North Whitehead*, op. cit., pp. 385-386.

16.   *Is It Too Late? A Theology of Ecology*, op. cit.

17.   Ibid., p. 93.

18.   Schubert Ogden, "The Reality of God," reprinted in Ewert H. Cousins (ed.), *Process Theology: Basic Writings by the Key Thinkers of a Major Western Movement* (New York; Paramus; Toronto: Newman Press, 1971), p. 119.

19.   *Process and Reality*, op. cit.

20.   "The Reality of God," op. cit., p. 121.

21.   Ibid., p. 123.

22.   Ibid., pp. 125-126.

23.   Ibid., p. 123.

24.   Edward Schillebeeckx, *God, the Future of Man* (London: Sheed and Ward, 1969).

25.   Pierre Teilhard de Chardin, *Man's Place in Nature*, tr. René Hague (New York: Harper & Row, 1966), p. 29. The book starts with the sentence: "Man is a part of life."

26.   Ibid., p. 17.

27.   Ibid., p. 18.

28.   Ibid., p. 64. He develops this idea in a very interesting way. Where did the first Indian, or the first Chinese, or the first Greek come from? The origin of a nation, a civilization, well in the past, is unrecoverable.

29.   Ibid., p. 72.

30.   Ibid., p. 87.

31.   Ibid., p. 101.

32.   Ibid., p. 102.

33.   Ibid., p. 105.

34.   Ibid.

35.   Ibid., p. 106.

36. Ibid.
37. Ibid., p. 118.

CHAPTER FIVE

1. The (not very) critical edition of St. Basil is in S. Giet (ed.), "Basile de Césarée. Homélies sur l'Hexaemeron. Texte grec, introduction et traduction" in *Sources Chrétiennes 26* (Paris: Editions du Cerf, 1949). For an English translation, see *A Select Library of Nicene and Post-Nicene Fathers* (Grand Rapids, Mich.: Wm. B. Eerdmans, Series Two, Vol. 8), pp. 52-107.
2. Cf. Harold F. Cherniss, *The Platonism of Gregory of Nyssa* (Berkeley; London: University of California Publications in Classical Philogy, Vol. II, No. 1).
3. III:113B.
4. It is interesting to note that οὐρανὸς or heaven was the original name for the whole universe. The word κόσμος was a neologism introduced by Pythagoras (according to Diogenes Laertius VIII:48) and occurs for the first time in our documents in this sense in a fragment of Heraclitus. See A. E. Taylor, *A Commentary on Plato's Timaeus* (Oxford: Clarendon Press, 1928), pp. 65 ff.
5. J. Moreau, *L'Ame du Monde de Platon aux Stoïciens* (Hildesheim: Olms, 1965). See especially pp. 166 ff.
6. The interesting question of how an unperishable world can have perishable parts was hotly debated in classical antiquity. See for examples Philo, *De Confusione Linguorum*, 34:173; *De Praem, et Poenit*, 7:42; *De Aeternitate Mundi*, 5:20, etc. Athenagoras, *Legat*, 16:17/18,20; 22:18/8-9; Eusebius, *Praep. Evang.*, III:10:3-4; Cicero, *De Natura Deorum* 1, 1:13,33, etc. For an extended discussion on the subject, see Jean Papin, *Théologie Cosmique et Théologie Chrétienne* (Paris: Presses Universitaires de France, 1964).
7. *The Platonism of Gregory of Nyssa*, op. cit., pp. 40 ff.
8. E. Mühlenberg, Die Unendlichkeit Gottes bei Gregor von Nyssa. Gregors Kritik am Gottesbegriff der klassischen Metaphysik: Forschungen zur Kirchen- und Dogmengeschichte, Vol. 16 (Göttingen: Vandenhoeck & Ruprecht, 1966). For a French summary of Mülenberg's thesis, see Charles Kannengieser, "L'infinité divine chez Grégoire de Nysse", in *Recherches de Science Religieuse*, Vol. LV (Paris: Aux Bureaux de la Revue, 1967), pp. 55-65.
9. Plato, *Parmenides*: 10(137d). Plato also makes clear that that which has no boundaries can have no parts.
10. *Physics* Δ :6, 207a.
11. Jaeger, et al., (eds.), *In Ecclesiasten VII. Gregorii Nysseni Opera*, Vol. V, pp. 4122/18-416/10. Engl. tr. author's.
12. H.-F. Weiss has rendered the great service of making a comparative study of the cosmologies of Hellenistic and Palestinian Judaism in *Untersuchungen zur Kosmologie des hellenistischen und palästinischen Judentumms* (Berlin: Akademie-Verlag, 1966).
13. G. Florovsky, *Creation in St. Athanasius* (Berlin: Akademie-Verlag, 1962), pp. 36-57.
14. See J. N. D. Kelly, *Early Christian Creeds*, second edition (London: Black, 1960), pp. 209-210.

15. The concept is further elaborated and documented in the author's unpublished dissertation, "God-World-Man Relationship in Gregory of Nyssa." Serampore: 1973. For a full and lengthy discussion of the concept of *diastema*, see also the unpublished manuscript by P. Dandelot, "La Doctrine du Diastema chez Saint Grégoire de Nysse." Louvain: 1960.

16. For a full discussion of the notion of participation, see Fr. David Balas, *Metousia Theou: Man's Participation in God's Perfection according to St. Gregory of Nyssa*, Studia Anselmiana 55 (Rome: Herder, 1966).

17. Plato, *Timaeus*, 49a and 51a.

18. *Enneads* III:6,7.

19. *Hexaemeron*, Prooemium PG 44:69A. Engl. tr. author's.

20. This was pointed out by E. C. Messenger, *Evolution and Theology — The Problem of Man's Origin* (London: Burns, Oates & Washbourne, 1931). See especially pp. 23-26, 121-144. The book created quite a stir, at least in the English-speaking Roman Catholic world, and a sequel containing responses to it was published in 1950: E. C. Messenger (Ed.), *Theology and Evolution* (London: Sands & Co., 1950). See especially pp. 12-21, 87-101.

21. For a discussion of *conspiratio* and related concepts in Gregory, see J. Daniélou, *L'être et le temps chez St Grégoire de Nysse* (Leiden: E. J. Brill, 1970).

22. *De Hominis Opificio* 8, PG44: 148b.

23. *De Anima et Resurrectione*, PG46: 125c ff.

24. *Oration Catechetica* 6, PG4: 25D, 28A.

25. Ibid., 5, p. 27.

26. Ibid., 6, pp. 28/15 ff.

27. Ibid., 8, pp. 41 ff.

28. *De Hominis Opificio* 2, PG 44: 133B.

29. *De Hominis Opificio* 16, PG 44: 185B-D.

30. Ibid., 22, PG 44: 205C.

31. R. Gillet, "L'homme divinisateur cosmique dans la pensée de St Grégoire de Nysse" in *Studia Patristica*, Vol. VI, Texte und Untersuchungen, Vol. 81 (Berlin: Akademie-Verlag, 1962), pp. 62-83.

32. The equivalent *assimilation* is too passive to bring out the full sense of *exhomoiosis*, which means the working out of a potential likeness.

33. *Adespoton* means "not determined by an external master", hence self-determining.

34. *De Anima et Resurrectione*, PG 46: 10C-104A.

35. *De Hominis Opificio* 16, PG 44: 184A-B.

36. Ibid., 27, PG 44: 225D ff.

37. Ibid., 9, PG 44: 149B.

38. J. Daniélou draws attention in a note to the French translation of *De Hominis Opificio* (*Sources Chrétiennes* 6, op. cit., p. 94) to how Gregory differs substantially from Augustine in taking freedom rather than intelligence as constituting the image of God.

39. Gregory has picked up from Cicero the interesting idea that it is the liberation of the forelimbs that makes the mouth capable of language. Cf. Cicero, *De Natura Deorum* 151; Gregory, *De Hominis Opificio* 8, PG 44: 148C-D.

CHAPTER SIX

1. Hans Urs von Balthasar, *Liturgie Cosmique* (Paris: Aubier Montaigne, 1947).
2. Lars Thunberg, *Microcosm and Mediator. The Theological Anthropology of Maximus the Confessor* (Lund: Gleerup, 1965).
3. Hans Urs von Balthasar, *Présence et pensée* (Paris: 1942). E. v. Ivanka, "Vom Platonismus zur Theorie der Mystik" in *Scholastik, Vierteljahresschrift für Theologie und Philosophie*, XI (Freiburg: Herder, 1936), pp. 163-195.
4. *Ambigua*, PG 91: 1081 AB.
5. *Liturgie Cosmique*, op. cit., p. 95.
6. *Mystagogia* 7, PG 91: 685 BC.
7. *Microcosm and Mediator*, op. cit., pp. 396 ff. See *Ambigua* 41, PG 91:13312 B; *Quaest. ad Thalass* 48, PG 90:436 B.
8. *Ambigua* 5, PG 91:1056 AB.
9. Only some parts of Solovyev's nine-volume writings in Russian have so far been translated into Western languages. See, for example, S. L. Frank (ed.), *A Solovyev Anthology* (London: SCM Press, 1950); Vladimir S. Solovyev, *Lectures on God-Manhood*, introduced by P. P. Zonboff (London, Dublin: Fernhill, 1948; *God, Man and Church: The Spiritual Foundations of Life*, tr. by Donald Atwater (Cambridge: James Clarke & Co., 1937, 1974); *La crise de la philosophie occidentale* (Paris: Aubier Montaigne, 1947); *La justification du bien* (Paris: Aubier Montaigne, 1939).
10. *A Solovyev Anthology*, op. cit., p. 58. Solovyev's idea of humanity as some sort of world-soul has been studied by Edith Klum in *Natur, Kunst und Liebe in der Philosophie Vladimir Solo'evs Eine religionsphilosophische Unternehmung* (Munich: Verlag Otto Sagner, 1965). See especially chapter 1:6.
11. *A Solovyev Anthology*, op. cit., pp. 178-179.
12. See, for example, Fr. Georges Florovsky's article on "The Idea of Creation in Christian Philosophy"in *Eastern Churches Quarterly (VIII, 1949):25 ff;* Paul Evdokimov, "Nature" in *Scottish Journal of Theology* (Vol. 18, No. 1, 1965); Alexander Schmemann, *The World as Sacrament* (London: Darton, Longman and Todd, 1966); Olivier Clément, *Transfigurer le temps* (Neuchâtel, Paris: Delachaux et Niestlé, 1959; *idem.*, "L'homme dans le monde" in *Verbum Caro*, Vol. XII:45, 1958, pp. 4-22.
13. "L'homme dans le monde" in *Verbum Caro*, op. cit., pp. 11-12.

CHAPTER SEVEN

1. *Civilisation Technique et Humanisme*, Colloque de l'Académie Internationale de Philosophie des Sciences, Beauchesne, Paris, 1968, in Bibliothèque des Archives de Philosophie, Nouvelle Série No. 6.
2. Ibid., pp. 5-6 in Introduction by S. Dockx, secretary of the Académie Internationale de Philosophie des Sciences. English translation by present author.
3. I speak thus about Professor Polanyi on the basis of "personal knowledge" of him as a revered and beloved teacher to whom I owe much. His main works are *Personal Knowledge: Towards a Post-Critical Philosophy* (Chicago: University of Chicago Press, 1958); *The Tacit Dimension* (New York: Doubleday, 1967).
4. Paul Evdokimov, "Nature" in *Scottish Journal of Theology* (Vol. 18, No. 1, March 1965): 9.

CHAPTER EIGHT

1. Most Western futurologists are reluctant to acknowledge their indebtedness to Marxism at this point. See, for example, Polak, *The Image of the Future*, op. cit., Vol. II, pp. 172-173, where only passing reference is made to Karl Marx's insistence that the future can be known and predicted.

2. M. Maruyama and J. A. Dator (eds.), *Human Futuristics* (Honolulu: Social Science Research Institute, University of Hawaii, 1971), p. 1.

3. *The Image of the Future*, op. cit., Vol. I, p. 43. "It is a main thesis of this work that, for the first time in three thousand years of western civilization taken as a whole, such an obvious, almost universal and mass-scale loss of capacity or even of our will for equivalent substitution and innovation has taken place...There is a contraction of time-consciousness to the momentary present and a blurring of a specific sense of the future."

4. Ibid., p. 55.

5. Olivier Reiser, *Cosmic Humanism: A Theory of the Eight-Dimensional Cosmos Based on Integrative Principles from Science, Religion and Art* (Cambridge, Mass.: Schenkman Publishing Co., 1966).

6. Ibid., p. 448.

7. Ibid., p. 471.

8. Freeman J. Dyson, "Innovations in Physics", *Scientific American* (Vol. 199, September 1955).

9. Reprinted in the *International Herald Tribune* (Paris, 12/13 January 1974), under the heading "Ex-Astronaut on ESP".

10. Ibid.

11. Carlos Castaneda, *The Teachings of Don Juan. A Yaqui Way of Knowledge* (Harmondsworth: Penguin Books Ltd., 1973); *Journey to Ixtlan* (Harmondsworth: Penguin Books Ltd., 1974); *Tales of Power* (Harmondsworth: Penguin Books Ltd., 1976).

12. Lawrence Foss, "Does Don Juan Really Fly?", *Philosophy of Science* (Vol. 40, No. 2, June 1973): 298-316.

13. Ibid.

14. L. Feinberg, "Firewalking in Ceylon," *Atlantic Monthly* (May 1959).

15. "Does Don Jean Really Fly?", op. cit., p. 302.

CHAPTER NINE

1. It is for this reason that Eastern spirituality cannot follow an "obedience ethics such as Calvinistically-oriented theologians seek to derive from concepts like "the Lordship of Christ", "the sovereignty of God", or the "love commandments".

2. See Chapter One, 1. *The Present Impasse.*